PAGE
TO
STAGE

D0242633

This book is due for return on or before the last date shown below.

IN MEMORY OF KENNETH McLEISH

A Nick Hern Book

Ibsen's A Doll's House – Page to Stage
first published in Great Britain in 2007
as a paperback original by Nick Hern Books Limited,
14 Larden Road, London W3 7ST

Ibsen's A Doll's House
copyright © 2007 by Stephen Unwin

Page to Stage series
copyright © 2007 by Nick Hern Books Limited

Stephen Unwin has asserted his right
to be identified as the author of this work

Cover design: www.energydesignstudio.com

Typeset by Country Setting, Kingsdown, Kent CT14 8ES
Printed and bound in Great Britain by Bookmarque,
Croydon, Surrey

A CIP catalogue record for this book is available
from the British Library

ISBN 978 1 85459 872 1

The edition of *A Doll's House* quoted throughout
is the translation by Kenneth McLeish published
in the Drama Classics series by Nick Hern Books:
copyright © 1994 by Kenneth McLeish

The Page to Stage Series

Written by established theatre professionals, the volumes in the *Page to Stage* series offer highly accessible guides to the world's best-known plays – from an essentially theatrical perspective.

Unlike fiction and poetry, the natural habitat of the play is not the printed page but the living stage. It is therefore often difficult, when reading a play on the page, to grasp how much the staging can release and enhance its true meaning.

The purpose of this new series, *Page to Stage*, is to bring this theatrical perspective into the picture – and apply it to some of the best-known, most performed and most studied plays in our literature. Moreover, the authors of these guides are not only well-known theatre practitioners but also established writers, giving them an unrivalled insight and authority.

Contents

From Page to Stage

When we read and study plays, we sometimes forget that the playwright wrote them to be performed. The point of this book, therefore, is to show how the words on the page can be read as a guide to the way the action unfolds on the stage and, in particular, how one of the most influential plays ever written, Henrik Ibsen's *A Doll's House*, can be read as a work specifically conceived for the theatre.

To do this we need, first, to assemble the basic facts of Ibsen's life, and understand how the play relates to the rest of his work. We need to investigate his intentions, above all when it comes to the question of feminism; although it's impossible to ensure that these intentions are realised on stage (modern theatregoers have different views of the world from those of Ibsen's original audience[1]), a strong grasp of them is essential if we're to understand how the play was put together in the first place – and what it can say today.

It's also important to see Ibsen's masterpiece in a broader context, so we'll want to gain some knowledge of the world in which his play is set – in this case, middle-class life in late nineteenth-century Norway – and understand something of the beliefs and codes that governed it. Again, this may take us to surprising places and won't result in definitive knowledge, but it will, at least, help us to approach the play with some of the care and respect that it deserves.

Third, we should understand the idiom in which Ibsen was writing, particularly the nineteenth-century movement known as 'naturalism'. We need to get a sense of the theatre he was reacting against, as well as examining the aims of the naturalist movement as a whole. And in doing this we should remember that the heightened poetic quality of Ibsen's drama is a long way from modern realism.

Fourth, and most importantly, we need to examine the play's dramatic action, the unfolding story, in all its many twists and turns. Page and stage are inextricably linked and only a close reading of the entire text will allow us to imagine how it works in the theatre. And so we'll look for any clues that the playwright has given about how he imagined it in performance. We'll want to study the stage directions and try to picture the effect that Ibsen is trying to create.

The story of the play can only be convincingly told when it's inhabited by three-dimensional, living people, and so we need to examine the play's characters in detail, their fears and wishes, their strengths and weaknesses, their individuality and unpredictability. This should be based on a careful study of the long chain of events that each character has lived through before the action begins – their 'backstories' – but will also require insight into what drives them still.

Finally, since naturalism attempts the presentation of a dramatic illusion of real life, a study of *A Doll's House* requires a detailed understanding of its physical setting and scenery. This means attention to more than simply the walls and the doors, the windows and the floors; it's the furniture and fittings, the stove and letter box, the props and bric-à-brac that convey so much. And we need to consider what clothes the characters should be wearing, to indicate not simply their psychological make-up, but also their class, financial resources, status and style, as well as think about the lighting, sound effects and music that the play requires. *A Doll's House* was written to be performed in the theatre, and this book will try to return it to its true home.

This book doesn't pretend to be a definitive guide to how *A Doll's House* should be staged. Since there are so many imponderables – the scale of the theatre, the range of actors available, the talent and skill of those involved, the budget and so on – and each new group of artists inevitably brings its own perspectives to a production, it's unwise to attempt to be prescriptive. Instead, I've tried to concentrate on what Ibsen himself has specified, secure in the knowledge that creative and intelligent people will want to interpret this information in their own way. The theatre continuously reinvents itself, from generation to generation, and this book exists above all to help make that happen.

Henrik Ibsen

IBSEN'S LIFE (1828–1906)

Henrik Johan Ibsen was born on 20 March 1828 in the small town of Skien in south-east Norway. His mother came from a wealthy family and his early life was comfortable. However, in 1835, when Ibsen was seven, his father went bankrupt and he spent the rest of his childhood living on a farm in poverty. At the age of 18 he became an apprentice to an apothecary and caused a scandal by fathering an illegitimate son.

In 1849, aged 21, Ibsen wrote his first full-length play, the five-act verse tragedy, *Catiline*, which was published under a pseudonym. The following year he moved to Christiania (now Oslo) to study medicine, but failed to secure a place at the university. Instead he published a weekly magazine, consisting largely of social criticism and satire, and his one-act play, *The Burial Mound*, received a simple staging.

In 1851 Ibsen was appointed playwright-in-residence and resident stage director at the National Theatre in Bergen, which had been recently established to provide a home for emerging Norwegian drama. There he wrote four plays on Scandinavian subjects: *St. John's Night* (1853), *Lady Inger* (1855), *The Feast at Solhaug* (1856), and *Olaf Liljekrans* (1857). In 1857 he became Artistic Director of the Norwegian Theatre in Christiania, where he wrote *The Vikings at Helgeland* (1858), *Love's Comedy* (1862) and *The Pretenders* (1863). He married Suzannah Thoresen in 1858 and their son Sigurd was born a year later. In the same year he founded *The Norwegian Company* – a magazine dedicated to Norwegian art and culture – and travelled throughout Western Norway, collecting Scandinavian folksongs and folktales.

These early years in Christiania were difficult for Ibsen, and both the press and the theatre's board felt that he didn't fulfil his duties properly. In 1862 the theatre went bankrupt and in 1864, at the age of 36, Ibsen was given a grant to travel to Italy, which marked the beginning of his twenty-seven years abroad. In 1864, he began to write a play about Julian, a character from antiquity, which he finished in 1873, when it was published as *Emperor and Galilean*. In 1866, he wrote the dramatic poem *Brand*, his first real success, and the following year a second dramatic poem, *Peer Gynt*, which, with its focus on the dissolution of an individual's personality, marks the key breakthrough in his early work.

Ibsen and his family lived all over mainland Europe, moving to Dresden in 1868, Munich in 1875, Rome in 1878, and back to Munich in 1885. He travelled to Egypt in 1869 to witness the opening of the Suez Canal, and spent several summers in Gossensass in the Tyrol. With his move to Germany came a change in writing style as he turned his attention to the lives of the contemporary bourgeoisie and started out on his great cycle of realistic dramas. *The League of Youth* appeared in 1869 and *Pillars of the Community* in 1877. In Rome and Amalfi, he wrote his first masterpiece, *A Doll's House*, in 1879. This marked the beginning of a cycle of twelve great naturalistic plays, the body of work on which his reputation rests. *Ghosts* followed in 1881 and *An Enemy of the People* in 1882. In 1884 he wrote *The Wild Duck* ('the master's masterpiece', as it has been called), followed by *Rosmersholm* (1886) and *The Lady from the Sea* (1888). In 1889 he met two young women, Emilie Bardach and Helene Raff, and his apparently platonic relationships with these two muses affected much of his subsequent work. It was in this period that his plays began to be performed throughout Europe and America. In 1890, he wrote *Hedda Gabler*, the last he wrote in exile.

In July 1891, aged 63, Ibsen moved back to Norway and settled in Christiania, where he wrote *The Master Builder* (1892), *Little Eyolf* (1894), *John Gabriel Borkman* (1896) and the dramatic epilogue *When We Dead Awaken* (1899). These late plays focus on the complex relationships between old age and youth, art and life, and face up to the inevitability of death with tremendous honesty. In the last years of his life, he was an international figure, much fêted and honoured, both in Norway and abroad. In 1900, he suffered the first of a series of strokes that prevented him from writing, and he died in Christiania on 23 May 1906.

IBSEN'S THEATRE

Although Ibsen blossomed as a playwright comparatively late in life, he showed a fascination with the stage from his youth. His mother was interested in the theatre, and the young Henrik locked himself away and staged plays in a miniature puppet theatre; he also inherited his mother's love of art and enjoyed painting and drawing. However, his father was brutal, even by the standards of the time, and contemporary accounts suggest that Henrik was a withdrawn, shy young man, though with a deeply-rooted sense of comic mischief.

Ibsen's formal education was limited and, as an assistant pharmacist, he had no opportunities to go to the theatre. However, he read a great deal: Shakespeare, Schiller, the Danish dramatists Ludvig Holberg and Adam Oehlenschlager, as well as the Icelandic sagas, Scandinavian folk mythology, the Greek and Latin classics and, of course, the Bible. All this was to have a profound impact on his later work, where this literary background can often be glimpsed beneath the surface. His juvenile writing, however, tends to be rather satirical – and sketchy – in quality.

In Ibsen's youth there were no permanent professional theatres in Norway, only Danish (and a few Swedish) touring companies, and the Norwegian theatre was a pale reflection of mainstream Danish taste and tradition. However, this was the great period of European nationalism, especially in the smaller states, and Bergen and Christiania both saw attempts to create an indigenous 'national' theatre. However, despite the attempts by the young Ibsen and others to write poetic drama that could give Norway its answer to Shakespeare, the repertoire of these new theatres was almost entirely foreign, dominated by translations of French commercial drama and its German and Danish imitations. The key figures were the French dramatists, Eugène Scribe (1791–1861) and his successor Victorien Sardou (1831–1908), who mastered the art of the 'the well-made play' (*la pièce bien faite*) – glossy and effective dramas, written in prose, carefully constructed and driven by strict logical development in plotting and motivation, but lacking in philosophical or psychological depth.

Ibsen's time in the professional theatre was to have a decisive influence on his later development, and it's important to realise that – like Shakespeare and Molière before him – Ibsen was a practical man of the theatre. He directed a large number of productions, worked with many actors and actresses, and watched hundreds of performances. He also became familiar with the everyday challenges, both managerial and artistic, of working in the theatre and putting on plays. In other words, by the time he had decided what he wanted to say and how he wanted to say it, he had acquired a thorough knowledge of the means at his disposal.

Within the space of two years came two key moments in Ibsen's development. The first was his departure from Norway for southern Europe in 1864, which, he said, 'left its mark on all my later work . . . [it was like] a feeling of being released from darkness into the light, escaping through a tunnel from mists into sunshine'. Nine of Ibsen's finest plays were written abroad, and an ambivalent attitude towards his native land runs through all of them.

The second was Ibsen's renunciation of poetic, nationalist drama and his decisive turn towards naturalistic plays written in prose. This absorbed all the lessons of the 'well-made play' but took it to a new pitch of psychological and philosophical intensity. It also, in the words of Ibsen's friend, the Danish critic Georg Brandes, 'subjected problems to debate'. Ibsen recalled his conversion in a letter in 1883:

> Verse has done the art of drama immeasurable harm. An artist of the theatre, with a repertoire of contemporary dramatic work, should not willingly speak a line of verse. Verse will scarcely find any application worth mentioning in the drama of the near future. In the last seven or eight years I have hardly written a single line of verse; instead I have exclusively studied the incomparably more difficult art of writing in the straightforward honest language of reality.[2]

NATURALISM

Ibsen has inevitably been linked to the revolution in naturalist theatre associated with Stanislavsky and his pioneering productions of Chekhov at the Moscow Art Theatre. While it's accurate to see Ibsen as part of the same movement, it should be pointed out that *A Doll's House* premiered in 1879, seventeen years before the first (disastrous) staging of *The Seagull*, and a full nineteen years before Stanislavsky's production of the play and the establishment of the Moscow Art Theatre in 1898.

Of course, Ibsen was part of a much broader movement, also occurring in the novel and in fine art which had its roots in the scientific notion that human beings are shaped above all by their environment – climate, food, living conditions, etc – and that the Romantic notion of the solitary individual standing aloof from the material world was a dangerous illusion.[3] However, *A Doll's House* was an early, pioneering work which was to have an enormous impact on the subsequent development of naturalisim in the theatre. Indeed, it was as a direct result of *A Doll's House* and *Ghosts*, Ibsen's second masterpiece, that André Antoine founded the Théâtre Libre in Paris in 1887, Otto Brahm opened the Freie Bühne in Berlin in 1889 and Jack Thomas Grein formed the Independent Theatre Group in London in 1891. All three were what we could call 'experimental' theatres, and devoted to the new naturalism.

Naturalistic theatre was made possible by technical advances, although its nineteenth-century manifestation would strike modern theatregoers as highly artificial. But the extent of the revolution shouldn't be underestimated. The Théâtre Libre invented the notion of the 'fourth wall' – instead of showing that they were aware of the audience, the actors imagined a fourth wall to the room, sealing off the stage from the auditorium – and used real materials in their productions: furniture, food, and even fountains. Real doors and windows were constructed, and set into painted canvas scenery. Costumes came to be seen as a way of reflecting contemporary 'character', and many actors took to wearing their own clothes on stage. The invention of electric lighting in the 1880s transformed what was possible: electric lights could be focused and were more flexible than gas. Make-up had to adjust to the subtler lighting and some of the melodramatic excesses of face-painting began to go out of fashion. The hardest struggle, however, was to change the acting style. This had been somewhat stentorian and declamatory, favouring stylised gestures and poses over the fine detail that the new theatre demanded.

The truly radical aspect of naturalism, however, lay not in its technical achievements but in the decision to tackle subjects which hitherto had been regarded as unworthy of artistic attention. Naturalist writers wrote about money and the role that it plays in society, and the grubby business of debt, banking, mortgages and wills. They wanted to show how people are shaped by the work they do and the conditions in which they live, and were interested in portraying the everyday experiences of the lower-middle and working classes. Most shockingly for polite society, they understood the centrality of sexuality in human experience and were prepared to address this taboo subject with a frankness which had been unthinkable thirty years earlier. What's more, the naturalists were prepared to write about the complexity of relationships between men and women, and, as Ibsen does so brilliantly in *A Doll's House*, contemplate the limits of marriage and the new role that women would play in the modern world.

It's important to stress that Ibsen's naturalism is in no way slavish. Despite a surface which is rich with everyday objects and actions, the plays are laced with symbolism (a tendency which becomes increasingly marked in the later plays), and, although the language is simple and the actions are real, it's more appropriate to think of Ibsen as writing a kind of 'poetic naturalism'. His cycle of naturalistic plays are dramatic art of the highest order – second, in my mind, only to Shakespeare – and beneath the surface lurks a whole catalogue of jostling theatrical and literary genres. Émile Zola's ringing declaration in his essay *Naturalism in the Theatre* (1881) – 'There is more poetry in the little apartments of a bourgeois than in all the empty, worm-eaten palaces of history' – is nowhere more triumphantly vindicated than in Ibsen's masterpieces.

BELIEFS

It's hard to overstate the impact of Ibsen's work on his contemporaries. By the mid 1880s (particularly following the furore caused by *A Doll's House*), each new play was eagerly awaited and performed almost immediately in all the important theatres of Europe and America. By the time he eventually returned to Norway in 1891 he was a celebrity and a new term, Ibsenism, had been coined to describe the movement to which his plays gave rise. The day of his funeral in 1906 was one of national mourning.

Ibsen can fairly claim to be one of the great dramatists of modern life – to be placed alongside Chekhov, Brecht and Arthur Miller – and his plays examine peculiarly contemporary questions with surgical precision. In all of his mature work his central subject is the same: the painful struggle for the truth to be spoken. In a letter he wrote: 'I believe that none of us can do anything other or anything better than realise ourselves in spirit and in truth'. This struggle exists in many areas, personal as well as social, and takes place between the individual, on his or her path of self-realisation, and the claims of society, with its emphasis on duty to others. Ibsen never loses touch with the pain that's caused by the pursuit of that self-realisation, and the destruction that is its inevitable consequence; at times, particularly in the later plays, it's almost as if he's warning against it. However, with a powerful instinct for tragedy, he shows that this process of self-realisation is inevitable if society and the individual are to be reformed.

At first, Ibsen was regarded as an issue-based writer, a dramatist whose plays addressed the big social questions of his time. This was certainly the view of one of his earliest champions, the Irish playwright and critic George Bernard Shaw. However, to think of Ibsen as a mere moraliser is simplistic: his vision is tougher, and much more austere. He is the master dramatist who confronts his readers and audiences with the most fundamental of modern questions: how do we lead a meaningful life, if there is no God?

Writing 'A Doll's House'

Ibsen started to write *A Doll's House* in Rome in the spring of 1879. He completed the play in Amalfi (south of Naples) in the summer of the same year. You can still visit the room in the *Hotel Luna Convento* where he worked.[4] The weather was exceptionally hot, even for Southern Italy, yet there is a photograph of Ibsen standing stiffly, in full frock coat and tie, taking a walk along the seafront in the midday sun. We may wonder how he managed to write a masterpiece set during a Scandinavian Christmas at the height of an Italian summer.

IBSEN AND FEMINISM

A Doll's House is famous, above all, for the way that it shows a young woman gaining self-confidence and independence of mind in a highly conventional, male-dominated society. It is, without doubt, the single most important work of feminist fiction, and it's hard to think of a play that has been more revolutionary in its impact, as the American feminist, Kate Millett, wrote:

> In Aeschylus . . . one is permitted to see patriarchy
> confront matriarchy, confound it through the knowledge of
> paternity, and come off triumphant. Until Nora slammed
> the door announcing the sexual revolution, this triumph
> went nearly uncontested.[5]

The story of the play has its roots in a real-life episode. Ibsen's young protégée, Laura Kieler (the 'lark' as Ibsen used to call her), was trapped in an unhappy marriage. When her husband contracted tuberculosis, they took a long holiday to Switzerland and Italy, where he recovered. Returning via Munich, Laura confided in Ibsen's wife, Suzannah, that she had secretly borrowed the money for the trip and was now struggling to keep up with the repayments. Suzannah advised her to tell her husband the truth; when she did so, however, he was so furious that he drove her to a nervous breakdown, and subsequently had her committed to a lunatic asylum. This provided Ibsen with the kernel of the story of *A Doll's House* – even if he came up with a startlingly different ending.

Then, in January 1879, there was a row about the proposed appointment of a female librarian at the Scandinavian Circle in Rome, and Ibsen made a famous speech in her defence:

> Is there anyone in this assembly who dares to claim that our women are inferior to us in culture, intelligence, knowledge or artistic talent? I don't think many men would dare to suggest that. Then what is it men are afraid of? I hear that it is accepted tradition here that women are such clever intriguers that we keep them out because of this. Well, I have met with a good bit of male intrigue in the course of my life . . . What I am afraid of is men with small ambitions and small thoughts, small scruples and small fears, those men who devote all their ideas and all their energies to obtain certain small advantages for their own small and servile selves.[6]

Of course, Ibsen's stated commitment to the betterment of women's position in society was not entirely original. His friend Georg Brandes had translated John Stuart Mill's *The Subjection of Women* in 1869, and a discussion of women's rights was current in Scandinavian intellectual circles. Furthermore, the Norwegian writer, Camilla Collett, a friend of Ibsen's wife Suzannah, was a radical feminist who debated the seriousness of women's rights with Ibsen and may have influenced his thinking. Nevertheless, it is an extraordinary position for a middle-aged, middle class male to take in the 1870s.

However, while we shouldn't underestimate the huge impact the play had on the 'woman question' (as the nineteenth- and early twentieth-century debate about women's rights was sometimes called), it's equally dangerous to describe Ibsen's own intentions as 'feminist', and it's important that we do not see it only from a twenty-first century perspective. Nowhere does Ibsen argue for the flattening of sexual difference – let alone for the return of the matriarchy – or make broad claims for men's culpability or women's victimhood. Nor does he campaign for equal pay, birth control or votes for women.[7]

His point is more complex and, in many ways, more difficult to grasp, as is evident from his *Notes for a Tragedy for Today* (1878):

> There are two kinds of moral law, two kinds of conscience, one in man and a completely different one in women. They do not understand each other; but, in matters of practical living, the woman is judged by man's law as if she were not a woman but a man.

> The wife in the play ends by having no idea what is right and what is wrong; natural feeling on the one side, and belief in authority on the other lead her to utter distraction.

> A woman cannot be herself in modern society. It is an exclusively masculine society, with laws made by men, and with prosecutors and judges who judge feminine conduct from the masculine standpoint.

> She has committed forgery, and it is her pride; for she did it for love of her husband, and to save his life. But this husband, full of everyday rectitude, stands on the basis of the law and regards the matter with a masculine eye.

> Soul-struggles. Oppressed and bewildered by belief in authority, she loses her faith in her own moral right and ability to bring up her children. Bitterness. A mother in the society of today, like certain insects, ought to go away and die when she has done her duty towards the continuance of the species. Love of life, of home, of husband and children and kin. Now and then a womanlike shaking off of cares. Then a sudden return of apprehension and dread. She must bear it all alone. The catastrophe approaches, inexorably, inevitably. Despair, struggle and disaster.[8]

Thus it seems that Ibsen's aim in *A Doll's House*, rather like Sophocles' in his *Antigone*, was to show how men and women operate in entirely different ways, and that a woman finds it impossible to be herself in late nineteenth-century bourgeois society because of the dominance of man-made laws and conventions. The outcome, he stresses, has a tragic necessity to it, and Nora's final departure is full of apprehension and regret –

as anyone whose marriage has failed knows. Furthermore, we should remember that the play makes its impact through two different couples[9] – one of whom separates, while the other is brought together – and that it is in the combination of these two complementary perspectives that its deeper meaning lies.

Twenty years after *A Doll's House* was written, Ibsen made a speech to the Norwegian Women's Rights League:

> I am not a member of the Women's Rights League. I have never been deliberately tendentious in anything I have written. I have been more of a poet and less of a social philosopher than people generally seem inclined to believe. I thank you for your good wishes, but I must decline the honour of being said to have worked for the women's rights movement. I am not even very sure what women's rights actually are. To me it has been a question of human rights. And if you read my works carefully you will realise that. Of course it is incidentally desirable to solve the problem of women: but that has not been my whole subject. My task has been the portrayal of human beings.

Of course, by the time Ibsen said these words his views may well have changed, and, like any artist, he was anxious to avoid being pigeonholed; nevertheless, his emphasis on the whole of humankind places his work beyond the narrow limits of revolutionary feminism which has sometimes been claimed for it.

TRANSFORMATION AND REBIRTH

At the very heart of *A Doll's House* is a drama of human metamorphosis.

Ibsen was fascinated by the way that human beings are capable of radical change, and he recognised that such transformations are the fundamental precondition for what he called self-realisation. The play tracks five stories of separate individual change and roots them in profoundly grasped psychology:

Nora, from a doll wife into an independent woman

Torvald, from being the master of all he surveys into an abandoned husband

Mrs Linde, from being all alone in the world to having someone to whom she can dedicate her life

Krogstad, from a rejected villain into a man capable of generosity and love

Dr Rank, from being a seemingly carefree bachelor to a man on the brink of death, the most extreme transformation of all.

Each is vividly drawn and together they make up the central action of the play.

These transformations have even deeper echoes, however, and *A Doll's House* is also a parable of rebirth – most notably Nora, who is reborn into a new life – and reflects the Christian story that is enacted in the three days over Christmas during which the play is set. Although, like all of Ibsen, *A Doll's House* is written from a distinctly atheistic perspective, the biblical resonance is deliberate and should create a kind of shadow play behind the realistic characters that populate Torvald and Nora's apartment. Thus *A Doll's House* is a secular version of the Christmas story, and it's possible this is where the deepest meaning of Ibsen's extraordinary masterpiece can be found – or at least looked for.

THE WORLD OF THE PLAY

'The past is a foreign country', L.P. Hartley wrote. When we're studying a play from as alien a time and place as nineteenth-century Norway, we need to approach it with special caution and respect. Although the eventual aim should be to imagine the play as a modern piece of theatre that's vibrant and speaks to a present-day audience, it's essential that we gain a sense of just how peculiar the world of the play is. This isn't an academic issue: it'll have a direct impact on our understanding of what motivates the characters and of what's at stake for them.

Late nineteenth-century Christiania (now Oslo) was a small provincial fishing harbour, the capital of a backward, poor and almost entirely rural region of Sweden (Norway was not to become an independent state until 1905).[10] The last quarter of the nineteenth century saw mass emigration from this part of Scandinavia – mostly to North America – and the beginnings of industrialisation and nationalism.[11] Nevertheless, Norway was still largely cut off from the currents of mainstream European culture. Not only could it not compete with the great capital cities – London, Paris and Berlin – but its inhabitants lived according to different rules. Christiania was tiny, and everyone from the governing and professional classes knew each other, at least by repute. It was a society in which the family, and duty to the family, was regarded as all-important, where men had almost unlimited power over their wives, who were expected to concentrate on children and home-making. Most importantly, this was a strictly Lutheran world, where people were judged not by their parents, or their background, but by their actions and their deeds. Judgement was severe and final, but a belief in shared endeavour and ultimate salvation was widespread. In other words, Christiania in the 1870s was more like nineteenth-century Vancouver than Victorian London: this was frontier territory, where it was possible to make it to the top through hard work and a good reputation; but also where a single mistake – forging a signature, for instance – could cast you out of society forever.

IN PERFORMANCE

A Doll's House ('Et Dukkehjem' in Norwegian[12]) was premiered at the Royal Theatre in Copenhagen on 21 December 1879 with Betty Hennings playing Nora. The English critic Edmund Gosse reported that 'all Scandinavia rang with Nora's declaration of independence. People left the theatre, night after night, pale with excitement, arguing, quarrelling, challenging'. Performances quickly followed the next year in Stockholm, Christiania, Helsinki and Bergen.

In Berlin, Hedwig Niemann-Rabe, the actress playing Nora, refused to perform the last scene, saying, 'I would never leave my children'. As a result, Ibsen reluctantly wrote a new ending (a 'barbaric outrage' as he called it), in which Nora at the last moment (on seeing her children asleep) relents. Some German theatres adopted this, but when the original ending was reinstated, a 'missing fourth act' was supposedly discovered (in fact, written anonymously), in which Torvald visits Nora (who is now staying with the happily married Krogstad and Mrs Linde), and they are reunited.

Ibsen's original play was soon performed throughout Europe and America: Eleonora Duse played Nora in Italian (1893), Meyerhold directed the play in St Petersburg with Vera Kommisarjevskaya (1906), Max Reinhardt was responsible for a production at the Kammerspiele in Berlin (1917), and the astonishing Alla Nazimova raised audible gasps of recognition when she played the part in New York at the end of the First World War (1918).

The English langage premiere took place in Milwaukee – of all places – on 2 June 1882, under the title *The Child Wife*. The first London performance was of an adaptation called *Breaking A Butterfly* ('*A Doll's House* with Ibsen taken out' as Harley Granville-Barker called it) on 3 March 1884. There followed a reading of the play in Bloomsbury on 15 January 1886 with Karl Marx's daughter, Eleanor, as Nora, her husband Edward as Torvald, William Morris' daughter as Mrs Linde, and Bernard Shaw as Krogstad. Havelock Ellis, who was in the audience, wrote:

> The great wave of emancipation which is now sweeping across the civilised world means nothing more than that women should have the right to education, freedom to work, and political enfranchisement – nothing in short but the bare ordinary rights of an adult human creature in a civilised state.

Eleanor Marx and Bernard Shaw subsequently did much to introduce Ibsen to British audiences.

The first full London performance took place on 7 June 1889 at the Novelty Theatre, in a translation by William Archer, with the American actress, Janet Achurch, as Nora (who reprised the part in 1893, 1897 and 1911). Granville-Barker described this as 'the dramatic event of the decade', but one critic spoke of:

> That foolish, fitful, conceited and unlovable Nora is to

drive off the stage the loving and noble heroines who have adorned it, and filled all hearts with admiration, from the time of Shakespeare to the time of Pinero.

This production was seen in the same year in New York.

Subsequent English-language Noras have included Ethel Barrymore (1905), Gwen Ffrangçon-Davies (1930), Lydia Lopokova (1934), Flora Robson (1939), Angela Baddeley (1946), Mai Zetterling (1953), Susan Hampshire (1972), Claire Bloom (1973), Cheryl Campbell (1981), Anna Carteret (1988), Kelly Hunter (1994), Janet McTeer (1996), Anne-Marie Duff (2000) and Tara Fitzgerald (2004).

Several films have been made of the play, the first a black-and-white silent version in 1911. Patrick Garland directed the play for television in 1973 with Claire Bloom, Anthony Hopkins, Ralph Richardson and Denholm Elliott. Joseph Losey made a heavily feminist version also in 1973 with Jane Fonda as Nora and David Warner as Torvald. Ingmar Bergman, whose films were influenced by Ibsen,[13] directed a radical version of the play at the Royal Dramatic Theatre in Stockholm (1989), a production which has been regularly revived.

The German director Rainer Werner Fassbinder's film *Nora Helmer* (1974) recast Nora as a careerist who doesn't leave the home but seizes power in it. The Austrian dramatist Elfriede Jelinek wrote a startling sequel to Ibsen's play called *What Happened After Nora Left Her Husband* (1980).

TRANSLATIONS

Writing in a small and obscure language, Ibsen's work has always relied on its translators. The best are those who have heeded Ibsen's stipulation that the plays should be translated into the everyday speech of ordinary people.

There are several major collected editions in English, all of which include *A Doll's House*: William Archer's *Collected Works* (1906–12), which is no longer in print; the authoritative *Oxford Ibsen* (1960–77), with its excellent notes and appendices (parts of which are still available in paperback); the straightforward, if rather stuffy, Penguin translations by Peter Watts and Una Ellis Fermor; and Michael Meyer's popular, but occasionally over-inventive, versions for Methuen. Best of all – in my opinion, at least – is Kenneth McLeish's outstanding translation of the play, which I directed for English Touring Theatre in 1994, with Kelly Hunter as Nora. This is published by Nick Hern Books in its Drama Classics series and is quoted throughout.

There are many one-off translations of *A Doll's House* (usually from literal translations by others), including those by Christopher Hampton (1971), Pam Gems (1980), Sean McCarthy (1982), Frank McGuinness (1996), Samuel Adamson (2003) and Bryony Lavery (2004).

FURTHER READING

George Bernard Shaw's *Quintessence of Ibsenism* (1891) provides a detailed – if opinionated – introduction to Ibsen's major plays, which tends to see them as 'Shavian' plays of ideas. Raymond Williams' *Drama From Ibsen To Brecht* (1969) provides a good summary, although from an explicitly political point of view. *The Cambridge Companion to Ibsen* (1994) brings together a number of fine scholars on various aspects of Ibsen studies, and Joan Templeton's *Ibsen's Women* (1997) is an outstanding study of the major plays from a sophisticated feminist perspective (including an excellent chapter on what she calls the 'male backlash' to *A Doll's House*). Frederick J. Marker and Lise-Lone Marker's *Ibsen's Lively Art* (1989) looks at the plays as pieces for the theatre. There are two major biographies of Ibsen in English – Michael Meyer's definitive *Ibsen* (1967–71) and Robert Ferguson's fascinating *New Biography of Ibsen* (1996) – both of which are rich in useful insights. Michael Pennington and I co-authored a *Pocket Guide to Ibsen, Chekhov and Strindberg* for Faber and Faber (2003) that introduces all the major plays of the three dramatists.

There are two books that concentrate on *A Doll's House*. Egil Törnqvist's *Ibsen: A Doll's House* provides a detailed history of how the play has been performed and thought about since its premiere (1995, as part of Cambridge University Press's

Plays in Production series), and Errol Durback's *A Doll's House: Ibsen's Myth of Transformation* (1991) examines the history and reception of the play in considerable detail.

Methuen's student edition comes equipped with useful notes, as does the Nick Hern Books Drama Classics edition, from which I have quoted in this book.

Backstory

One of the chief characteristics of A Doll's House – *and all of Ibsen's plays, in fact – is the slow revelation of what has happened before the action begins. This is sometimes called the backstory and understanding it in detail is essential to realising the meaning and drama of the play.*

The backstory is useful for two reasons: first, it helps actors see when their characters are hiding – or being confronted by – the truth; secondly, it gives a clear historical basis to their motivation. Thus, we'll need to gather as much information as we possibly can from the text and place it in chronological order, from the earliest episode right up to the moment the character walks onto the stage for the first time; it might even be a good idea to draw up a time-line, which shows the backstory in visual terms. And sometimes, we'll need to supplement the provable facts with our imagination.

NORA AND TORVALD

Nora and Torvald Helmer married eight years ago, and have since had three children (two boys and a girl). Torvald was a lawyer,[14] but soon after their wedding had a nervous break-down due to the pressure of work and had to stop. His doctors advised him to leave Norway and go south, to get away from the cold and enjoy the sun. However, they weren't well off and couldn't afford to go. When Nora discovered that his condition was more serious than the doctors had first suggested and that his life was in danger, she went to a moneylender, Nils Krogstad, to raise the cash to finance the trip. In a time when women weren't allowed to borrow money without their husband's permission, she had to do this without Torvald's knowledge. Furthermore, Krogstad would only lend it to her if her father guaranteed the repayments. He was on his deathbed, and rather than upsetting him, Nora forged his signature – shortly after he died. She also pretended to Torvald that her father had left them the money in his will.

The long holiday in Italy – probably in the Bay of Naples and on the Amalfi coast[15] – 'cost a fortune' but was strikingly successful. Since their return, says Nora, 'Torvald hasn't had a moment's illness. The children are fine, and so am I'. Furthermore, he's recently been appointed manager of the bank, a position that he will take up fully in the New Year, so the future is promising. Secretly, Nora has been paying Krogstad back what he is owed:

> Don't think it's been easy, meeting the payments on time, each time. Quarterly accounts, instalments – I can tell you all about that sort of thing . . . I saved a little bit here, a little bit there. Not much from the housekeeping, because of Torvald's position. The children couldn't go without nice clothes. Every penny he gave me for my little darlings, I spent on them . . . Every time Torvald gave me money for clothes, I put half of it away. I bought the simplest, cheapest things . . . Fortunately there were other things I could do. Last winter I was lucky: I got a lot of copying. I locked myself in every evening and sat and wrote, into the small hours.

Now the debt is just about to be paid off and she is finally:

> Free of it! I can play with the children . . . make the house pretty, make everything the way Torvald likes it. It'll soon be spring, the wide blue sky. We could have a holiday . . . the seaside. Free of it! I'm so happy, so happy.

MRS LINDE AND KROGSTAD

Kristine Linde (we're not told her maiden name) was at school with Nora but they haven't seen each other for at least nine years. Mrs Linde's husband died three years ago and didn't 'leave her enough to live on'. She has no children, 'not even sad memories'. However, as she confesses to Nora, she didn't love her husband and married him for other reasons: 'My mother was still alive: bedridden, helpless. I'd two younger brothers to look after. When he proposed, how could I not accept?' But the financial security he provided did not last:

'His business was shaky. After he died, it collapsed entirely. There was nothing left.' And since his death, she's been doing 'endless hard work' to support her dependents. Now, however, her mother is dead, her brothers are grown up and she has no responsibilities. So she's come to the city to get herself a job and give herself the chance of a new life.

Nils Krogstad slipped up some years ago. After he was sacked from a lawyer's firm for forging a signature, he started lending money on interest as a way of earning a living and bringing up his sons. He's regarded by society as a parasite and is regularly snubbed wherever he goes. He's now at a stage in life when he wants to change everything: he recently secured a junior position at the bank and thought he was clawing his way back into respectability. However, one of Torvald's first decisions on being appointed Bank Manager was to dismiss Krogstad because of his reputation. In his first scene with Nora, Krogstad makes his situation clear:

> But now I want done with it. My sons are growing up; for their sakes I want to be respectable again, as much as possible. That job at the Bank was the first step – and now your husband is kicking me down to the mud again.

Krogstad's desire to be 'respectable again' is his driving force and provides his motivation throughout the play.

Mrs Linde had a relationship with Krogstad several years ago, but left him for another man – her future husband – when he was in trouble. She told him in a letter. 'What else could I do?' she asks him now. 'I had to break with you. It was essential to kill everything you felt for me . . . I'd a bedridden mother and two small brothers. We couldn't wait for you, Nils. You'd no prospects then.' Her letter hurt Krogstad a great deal and deepened his feelings of rejection and failure. But now that Mrs Linde is free of her responsibilities, she feels 'empty. No one left to live for'. Krogstad's demonstration of the seriousness of his intentions allows Mrs Linde to remember the depth of her feelings for him, and leads to their reconciliation at the beginning of Act Three.

DR RANK

Rank's backstory is hard to ascertain, a reflection perhaps of his deliberately mysterious presence. It's evident that his father was a libertine who lived well and with little concern for standard morality. At some point Rank has realised that he is about to die; Ibsen implies that he's inherited syphilis from his father, although this is not made explicit in the text. It's also not entirely clear where his fortune comes from, or how busy he is as a practising doctor. It's likely that his money is inherited, not earned, and it's this, combined with his lack of dependants, that enables him to live in some style.

The Action

When thinking about how a play might look on stage, unfolding in three-dimensional space, it's essential that we read the text in the closest possible detail, alert to every clue about staging, character and dramatic action. And when a play is written by a dramatist with such meticulous theatrical imagination as Ibsen, it's doubly important that all our conclusions should emerge from such a study. And since Ibsen is the master dramatist of the repressed and the hidden, it's essential that we read the play not just for what's said, but for what's left unsaid, or only suggested obliquely.

This reading needs to be comprehensive and thorough, and we must look at the whole play, not just highlights. A common mistake is to focus on the most obviously dramatic moments – the tarantella, for example, or Nora's final departure – and neglect the 'less important' sections. If we do this, the production will lack context or three-dimensionality; worse still, the point of the play will be lost.

This chapter divides the three acts of the play into much shorter sections, usually marked by the arrival of a new character, but sometimes by a dramatic change of pace or atmosphere. These sections are designated merely for convenience, though they might coincide with the way the play is divided into 'units' for the purposes of rehearsal.

I've provided a detailed synopsis in roman *type and a commentary beneath in italics.*

Act One

Act One takes place on Christmas Eve.

I.

A bell rings in the hall, and we hear the front door being opened. Nora Helmer returns home from shopping: 'She is happy, humming a tune' and carries a number of parcels. In the doorway stands a Porter, 'carrying a Christmas tree and a basket', which he gives to Helene, the chambermaid. Nora tells her to hide the tree so that the children don't see it until it's 'trimmed'.[16] She gives the Porter a tip and he leaves. She closes the door, laughs to herself, takes two macaroons from a little bag and eats them, then listens carefully at the door of her husband's study.

This brief section immediately introduces us to several aspects of Nora's personality: her secretiveness, her financial generosity – at first sight, extravagance – and her affection for her children. It also sets up the contradiction between her happy, playful independence and the anxiety she feels about her husband.

The flat has an outer door that leads onto the shared staircase, but the room in which the action of the play takes place has a door of its own. In other words, the door into the room isn't the front door into the apartment. It's possible that when both are open we can see a flash of daylight beyond, in the stairwell.

2.

Having established that Torvald is at home, Nora resumes her humming and looks at her parcels. Torvald hears her and calls out through the study door, wondering when his 'little squirrelkin' came home. She asks him to come and see what she's bought. After a pause, he emerges, and asks if 'my little featherbrain has been spending all my money again?' She protests that this is the first Christmas they haven't needed to 'scrimp and save', adding that they could borrow money to tide them over until his first pay packet. He's appalled and lectures her on the perils of debt. When she becomes sulky, he gives her some housekeeping money, which she quickly pockets. She also shows him the children's Christmas presents, and hints at a surprise for him. But when she asks for some pocket money for herself, he dismisses her, saying that she'd only spend it on the housekeeping. They both agree that things will be better, now that the hard times are finally over.

In this section, we get our first glimpse of the play's central relationship. As we're to discover, Nora has been using the housekeeping money to pay off the secret loan from Krogstad, as well as

*providing for all the family, and has even managed to persuade
Torvald into thinking that she's extravagant. Her pretend sulkiness
and little-girl flirtatiousness are all part of an elaborate act that
she puts on to wheedle more money out of him, while his affec-
tionate but patronising replies demonstrate his blindness to what's
really going on. He finds her childishness erotic, and the more she
protests the more interested he becomes. Of course, all this must be
played subliminally: the surface is of an entirely 'normal' nineteenth-century bourgeois marriage. It's the tiny hints of what's
lurking beneath – the secrets – which provide the dramatic tension.*

3·

We hear the front doorbell ringing in the hall and the maid
announces the arrival of 'a lady, a stranger'. She also tells
Torvald that 'the doctor' (Rank) has gone straight through to
his study. As Torvald leaves Nora to join Rank, Mrs Linde
enters, in 'travelling clothes . . . timid and ill-at-ease'. At first,
Nora doesn't recognise her, but suddenly realises that she's
her old school friend, Kristine Linde. When Mrs Linde points
out that they haven't seen each other for nine or ten years,
Nora tells her how happy she's been in that time. Mrs Linde
has just arrived in town; Nora invites her to warm herself by
the stove. She tells her that she looks paler and thinner, and
suddenly remembers that Mrs Linde has lost her husband.
Mrs Linde explains that he left her too little to live on and that
she's had to work since his death. Tactlessly, Nora speaks of
her own good fortune – three healthy children and a husband
who has just got a well-paid job at the bank – but tells her that,
when they were first married, Torvald was very ill, so they
spent a year in Italy, which saved his life. She adds that it 'cost
a fortune', but implies that her father left them the money in
his will. Suddenly, realising that she's been talking only about
herself, Nora asks Mrs Linde whether it's true that she didn't
love her husband. Mrs Linde replies that she had no choice
but to stay with him and that after his death his business
collapsed entirely; since then she's been making her own way
('it's been endless hard work', she says, 'these last three
years'). When Nora tactlessly advises her to take a holiday, she
snaps: 'I've no daddy to pay the bills'.

The maid's announcement that Dr Rank has gone into Torvald's study (without anybody seeing him) indicates that it has two entrances: one from the living room and another from the hall. When Torvald goes to join Rank, he should leave through the door from the living room into the study.

Nora's failure to recognise Mrs Linde hints at her innate sense of superiority; but it also suggests that Mrs Linde has aged markedly. At first sight she's the polar opposite of Nora: an independent-minded woman who has had to work hard to look after her sick mother and young brothers and who now finds herself all alone in the world. But she reveals a deeper truth when she tells Nora that she feels 'empty', with 'no one left to live for'. When later we see the nature of her relationship with Krogstad, we come to understand more clearly what this means.

Mrs Linde's arrival is an important development in the unfolding drama. Her presence allows Nora to speak frankly about what she's been doing. Furthermore, her underestimation of Nora's situation triggers Nora into revealing more than she might do otherwise. It's important to note, however, that Nora doesn't reveal everything, including who lent her the money.

4.

Nora assures Mrs Linde that Torvald will help her, but when she patronises Nora for being a 'babe in arms', Nora says that she's not talked of her 'real problems'. So she leads her over to the sofa and says, 'The person who saved Torvald's life – it was me', explaining that she borrowed the money ('Four thousand, eight hundred kroner') herself, even though, as she says, 'a wife can't borrow without her husband's permission'. She also says that she hid from Torvald the seriousness of his condition, and persuaded him to take the break for her benefit. Mrs Linde wants to know if she'll ever tell him the truth, and Nora replies, 'with a light smile': 'One day. Perhaps. When I'm not quite such a pretty little thing.' She also explains how she's paying off the debt – by taking money out of the housekeeping, but also by taking on copying work – and says that she used to dream about a rich old man who would die and leave all his money to her. 'Now', she says, 'I'm free of it. I can play with the children . . . make the house pretty, make everything the way Torvald likes it. It'll soon be spring, the wide blue sky.'

Note the change in atmosphere when the two women move from the stool and the rocking chair by the stove (good for calm contemplation and memory) to the more comfortable sofa (good for more active and passionate discussion). Once moved, Nora is careful not to tell the whole sordid truth, that she borrowed the cash from a common moneylender (she doesn't know about Mrs Linde's involvement with Krogstad); instead she retreats into pleasure at her own cleverness. Her dream of a wealthy admirer makes Mrs Linde suspicious, but Nora's last exclamation gets to the heart of the relief she feels.

5.

The doorbell rings, and Mrs Linde decides that she should leave. Nora, however, tells her to stay. The maid announces that there's 'a gentleman here to see the master'. When Nora asks who it is, Krogstad appears at the door, and Nora surreptitiously ushers him into Torvald's study, through the hall door. Mrs Linde asks Nora about Krogstad and shows that she knows a surprising amount about him. But Nora doesn't want to talk about Krogstad and is pleased when Rank enters from the study.

This brief appearance of Krogstad raises the dramatic temperature. Not only is Nora alarmed by his arrival (what's he going to say to her husband?), but Mrs Linde, who is still in love with him, is disturbed to see him there too. Neither woman wants to share her secret with the other, and the audience is likewise in the dark. However, their reactions to his appearance should alert the audience to the fact that things are more complicated than they seem, without giving away exactly what those complications might be. It's important for the scene that Mrs Linde is positioned in such a way that Krogstad doesn't notice her when he comes in, but that she can see him, or at least hear his voice.

6.

Rank enters, sees Mrs Linde and feels that he shouldn't stay. Nora introduces them to each other: he says that he noticed her on the stairs earlier. Mrs Linde explains that she finds stairs difficult, and he presumes that she must be unwell; she says, however, that she's exhausted and has come to town to look for work: 'One has to live', she tells them ruefully. Rank agrees, saying that his patients all feel the same, including those who are 'morally sick', such as Krogstad. He speaks of how 'some people go round sniffing out weakness' and back the weak person into 'a profitable corner'. Mrs Linde is shocked by his cynicism, but Nora is excited by the prospect of Torvald's newly found power as bank manager. She tells Rank there is one thing she'd like to say 'straight out' to her husband, but that it's 'too terrible'. Hearing that Torvald is about to enter the room, Rank encourages her to speak, but she just hides the bag of macaroons she has been eating.

In this section we see Rank's curious combination of charm, cynicism and despair. Rank is, of course, the rich, dying man that Nora mentioned to Mrs Linde, as Mrs Linde realises. This is borne out by what happens: we see the familiarity of his relationship with Nora, which is mostly avuncular, but also flirtatious. His frankness about the proximity of death (his own included) and his almost jovial acceptance of the folly of trying to avoid it, give Nora a powerful sensation of the transience of all things – and this encourages her recklessness. His attempts to persuade her into talking to Torvald are more provocative than serious, but his condemnation of Krogstad has real force behind it – disturbing to both Nora and, more especially, Mrs Linde.

7.

Torvald comes out of his study, with his coat and hat, ready to go out, and Nora runs to him, keen to hear whether he's got rid of Krogstad. She introduces Mrs Linde as a 'genius at bookkeeping', and asks him to find her a job at the bank. He says that she 'could hardly have come at a better time' and he may well have something for her. However, he has to go to the bank, and Rank says that he'll join him. Mrs Linde says that she's going too, to find a room. As they leave, children's voices can be heard coming up the stairs: Torvald says, 'This'll soon be no place to be, except for mothers.'

Torvald's second entrance into the play should show another side of his character: a man with business affairs to get on with. He has been unyielding with Krogstad in his study and has sacked him (as we'll soon see), but is now magnanimous with Mrs Linde – whom he takes kindly to almost immediately. His exit with Rank and Mrs Linde should be full of businesslike bustle: picking up hats, coats and a briefcase, cracking cheerful jokes, and so on. It's made clear that the man's world lies outside and that the home is a sacred preserve for mothers and children. Mrs Linde – childless, hard-working, old before her time and alone – is accepted by the men, but only as an unthreatening junior.

8.

The three children, Ivar, Emmy and Bob, come running into the apartment with their nanny, Anne-Marie, and tell their mother what they have been up to outdoors, in the snow. Thrilled to see them with their rosy cheeks, Nora picks up her youngest and dances with him. When Anne-Marie starts to take their coats off, Nora intervenes and tells her to help herself to some coffee: she'll look after the children herself. Delighted to see their mother, the children all chatter excitedly, and she starts to play a game of hide-and-seek with them. When they insist that she should hide first, she takes refuge under the table; when they eventually discover her, they all shriek with delight.

This short scene is essential to the balance of the play. It demonstrates the depth of Nora's love for her children and the pleasure she takes in them. It also shows that she can be unconventional: taking over from the nanny, running around like a child and joining in the shrieking and giggling, playing hide-and-seek and hiding under a table herself. Of course, this is all quite natural in a modern family, but in a middle class nineteenth-century woman such behaviour would suggest a real independence of spirit; childish as it may be, this hints at the greater unconventionality that she demonstrates so conclusively later on. It also suggests a certain desperation, as if Nora foresees the possibility of losing her children.

Ibsen doesn't actually write the children's lines, and in a production these should be improvised. Of course, he asks for such a hubbub of laughing, giggling and general excitement that it should be difficult to catch everything they say.

9.

In the meantime, Krogstad has knocked at the hall door and quickly appears at the half-opened door. Nora is shocked to see him again and tells him that her husband is out. But he wants to talk to her, and so Nora 'gently' sends the children off to Anne-Marie, reassuring them that 'the man won't hurt Mummy'. She closes the door behind them and asks Krogstad what he wants, adding that 'It's not the first of the month' (when her payments are due). He says that he's just seen Torvald in the street with Mrs Linde – who, he says, was once a 'friend' of his – and wants to know if Mrs Linde has been given a job in the bank. When Nora confirms that she has ('One isn't without influence', she says), Krogstad tells her bluntly that he's been sacked and asks her to put this influence of hers to work for him, to help him keep his 'position of dependence in the bank'. He reminds her that a long time ago he 'slipped up', but he's now keen to become 'respectable again': the job at the bank was the first step, he says, but now Torvald is kicking him down 'into the mud again'. She's shocked to realise that Krogstad might tell her husband the truth about what she's been up to, and snaps at him: 'Do it, do it, and see where it gets you . . . You'll never get your job back.' Krogstad, however, reminds her of the facts: he lent her money on the condition that her father would guarantee the repayments. He points out that it appears her father signed the contract three days after he died – in other words, she must have forged the signature. When Krogstad speaks of the seriousness of what she's done and says that he'll show the document to the court, she's scornful:

> Nonsense. A daughter can't save her dying father from care and worry? A wife can't help her sick husband? I know nothing about the law, but there must be laws about that.

But Krogstad's reply as he leaves is full of threats: 'Do as you please, but remember one thing: If I lose everything a second time, you keep me company'.

Krogstad's appearance at the half-opened door while Nora plays with the children immediately sets the tone: in a thriller, the threat to the peaceful home always arrives at a moment of domestic bliss, and Krogstad's shadowy presence prompts Nora to usher her children off to safety. His description of being alone in a restaurant, seeing Torvald and Mrs Linde walk past together, gives us a vivid impression of his isolation, and his behaviour here shows just how desperate he is to rejoin society – at any cost. Nora's responses show a mixture of grandeur, naivety and growing panic. Her conviction that forging her father's signature was acceptable bears out Ibsen's point:

> There are two kinds of moral law, two kinds of conscience, one in man and a completely different one in women. They do not understand each other; but, in matters of practical living, the woman is judged by man's law as if she were not a woman but a man.[17]

It's important that the scene has dramatic tension but doesn't slip into melodrama: Krogstad's approach is logical, carefully thought through and not undertaken out of malice. It's the way that society has treated him – above all the rejection he faced for committing the same crime as Nora (forging a signature) – not any psychopathic tendencies, that makes him act as he does. It's also important that the actors play the scene with sufficient attention to detail so that the audience catches the vital information about Nora's crime. Krogstad's insistence on facts is very helpful in this regard.

10.

Left alone, Nora is lost for a moment in thought, but she soon shrugs it off ('Ridiculous. He was trying to scare me', she says to herself) and gathers up the children's clothes. After a moment of panic ('But suppose – ?'), she reassures herself ('No. I did it for love.'). The children re-emerge and ask if 'the man' has gone. They want to play another game but she refuses and sends them off again. She sits on the sofa and tries

to do some sewing. After a moment she goes to the hall door
and tells Helene to bring in the Christmas tree. She opens a
drawer, looks in it, and says 'I can't. I can't', but is interrupted
by Helene bringing in the tree. Nora tells her to put it in the
middle of the room and, left alone and distracted, starts to
decorate it:

> A candle here . . . Flowers here . . . That dreadful man. No,
> no, it's all right. The tree, the tree must be beautiful. Torvald,
> I'll do whatever you want. I'll sing for you, dance for you –

At which point, Torvald returns, with a case full of important
papers.

*After the long dialogue between Krogstad and Nora, this section is
deliberately broken up and full of physical movement, reflecting
Nora's restlessness, veering from confident domesticity to rising
panic. When she refuses to play with her children, we see the way
that Krogstad will come between her and them. Then, moments
later, Nora, sitting on her sofa and sewing, presents a picture of
domestic contentment; by contrast, although Ibsen doesn't tell us
what Nora can see in the drawer – is it a pistol? – it obviously
panics her. Instead she takes refuge in decorating the Christmas
tree and convinces herself that she'll be able to use her charms to
persuade Torvald to give Krogstad his job back.*

II.

Nora is surprised to see Torvald back so soon, and his first
question is a test: 'Has anyone called?' Nora denies it, but
Torvald says that he saw Krogstad at the gate and knows he
was trying to persuade her to put a word in for him and
pretend that it was her idea. He reprimands her for lying in a
way that's both patronising and playful. Saying that he wants
to hear nothing more about it, he sits by the stove and starts to
look at his papers. She gets his attention back by pretending to
be interested in the outfit that she's planning to wear at the
Boxing Day fancy dress party; she's much more interested in
his papers – the bank's review of staffing and duties, which he
has to have ready by New Year – but cannot find the right
moment to ask him to give Krogstad his job back. She asks

him what Krogstad had done that was so terrible. Torvald explains that a while back 'he forged someone's name', and that:

> An atmosphere like that, a stench of lies and deceit, poisons the whole household. Each breath children take in a house like that is a lungful of deadly germs.

He adds that 'almost always when people go bad young in life, the cause is a deceitful mother', but admits that 'Krogstad has been poisoning his children for years'. He insists that his 'little Nora' should never ask him to help Krogstad again: 'People like him literally make me ill.' He then gathers his papers and goes into his study, saying 'I must try to get through some of this before dinner. And there's your fancy dress to think about'.

Torvald has returned earlier than expected, in order to work on the review of the bank's staffing: an image of his new-found power and industry. Nora uses every feminine trick she can to gain influence over him but is surprised to be confronted by his obduracy. Hearing that Krogstad's crime was the same as hers shocks her deeply, and she's even more dismayed to hear Torvald's description of the damage inflicted on children by people like her. Throughout, however, she clings to the conviction that everything she did was out of love – for her father, her husband and her children – and is appalled to realise that she may have caused them damage.

12.

Left alone, Nora mutters to herself: 'It can't be. No. It can't.' Anne-Marie comes in to tell her that the children are crying out for her; but Nora doesn't want to see them, and tells Anne-Marie to stay with them. In the last moments of the Act, she's once again alone: 'Poison them?' she asks incredulously, 'My children, my family? Never. Impossible.'

Nora is dismayed at what Torvald has said, but she doesn't yet question the basis of his argument. Instead, she ends the Act utterly determined to resolve everything: persuade Torvald to give Krogstad his job back, be reunited with Torvald and her children, and be happy. The audience should end Act One sympathetic to Nora's position and admiring her determination, but sceptical as to whether she'll be able to surmount the obstacles that face her.

Act Two

Act Two takes place during the afternoon on Christmas Day: 'In the corner beside the piano, the Christmas tree stands stripped of its decorations, and with its candles burned to stumps.'

1.

Nora is alone in the apartment, restlessly pacing up and down. She picks up her evening cape, puts it down again, and convinces herself that someone is coming. She looks nervously at the locked letter box in the hall and is relieved that it is empty, consoling herself that Krogstad didn't mean what he said the previous day: 'Things like that don't happen', she says to herself, 'they don't. I've got three small children.'

Although it's Christmas Day, Nora, a wife and mother, is all alone. She's been out leaving a message for Mrs Linde. Having failed to persuade Torvald to give Krogstad his job back, she's anxiously awaiting the arrival of a letter from Krogstad that'll tell Torvald everything. Her insistence that the worst cannot happen to her is deliberately ironic, and we know that Krogstad will almost certainly carry out his threat.

2.

Anne-Marie enters with a large cardboard box full of fancy dress. When she points out that the item that Nora wanted needs mending, Nora replies: 'I wish I'd torn it to pieces.' She tells Anne-Marie that she's asked Mrs Linde to visit her and that she'll help. She wants to know about her children ('Are they asking for me?') but makes it plain that she doesn't want to see them ('I've no time any more'). She also asks Anne-Marie: 'D'you think if their Mummy went far away, they'd forget her?' And she wants to know how she, Anne-Marie, could give up her own child to be fostered. Anne-Marie says that she had no choice and needed to take the position as 'nurse to baby Nora', adding that, at the time, she was 'a poor girl in trouble'. Nora presumes that her daughter has 'long forgotten' her, but Anne-Marie's answer is stoical: 'No, no. She wrote to me, when she was confirmed, and when she got married.' Nora hugs her and recalls what a good mother she was to her when she was young, drawing some comfort from the knowledge that Anne-Marie will look after her children when she's gone, even though the last thought is unspoken: 'I know if my little ones had no one else, you'd . . .' Encouraged, she sends Anne-Marie back to the children, saying: 'Tomorrow you'll see how pretty I'll look.' Anne-Marie leaves, assuring Nora that she'll be 'the prettiest one' at the party.

This small scene between Nora and Anne-Marie gives us essential insights into Nora's past, as well as her current state of mind. Nora's appreciation of Anne-Marie looking after her as a child suggests that Nora's mother was not around in her childhood (perhaps she died in childbirth), and that she was brought up in a rather unconventional way. Anne-Marie's past is also revealing: she became pregnant by a man who would not or could not marry her, so she had to give her daughter up to be fostered. She needed to work for a living and was employed by Nora's father as a nanny; she loved Nora as if she was her own daughter (they were the same age) and looked after her in every way. Now, she's looking after Nora's children with the same love and devotion, and it's hardly surprising that Nora turns to her in her anxiety about their future.

3.

Alone again, Nora tries to convince herself that Krogstad isn't going to deliver his letter and attempts to think about something else; she even starts to count to ten aloud. Suddenly she hears someone at the door and gasps. She tries to go to the door, but cannot move. To her amazement, Mrs Linde comes in from the hall where she's taken off her coat, saying that she had heard that Nora wanted to see her. Nora explains that she needs some help repairing the outfit she wants to wear for the fancy dress party that her upstairs neighbours, the Stenborgs, are holding the next day; 'Torvald wants me to go [dressed] as a Neapolitan fishergirl, and dance the tarantella I learned in Capri.' Mrs Linde quickly sees what has happened to the dress ('It's easy. The frill's come undone, here and here') and starts to repair it. She thanks Nora for the 'lovely evening, yesterday', and asks whether Dr Rank is always so gloomy.

Nora tells her that he's 'seriously ill. Lesions in the spine', and suggests that it's the fault of his 'horrible' father: 'Woman after woman. That's why the son . . . Tainted blood.' Mrs Linde is amazed that Nora knows about these things and asks her if Rank comes to visit every day; she also suggests that Rank might not be all he seems. Nora reassures her, saying that Torvald encourages Rank to visit her, since they both enjoy gossip. But Mrs Linde dismisses this, and advises her to finish with Rank. She also recalls Nora's reference to a 'rich admirer' and says that she assumes that it must have been Rank who lent her the money for the Italian trip. Nora dismisses this, but says that if she did ever ask him for money she'd accept it, behind her husband's back. She also assures Mrs Linde that she'll soon 'finish with the other' (i.e. Krogstad), and suddenly asks her, 'When you pay off a debt, you get your contract back . . . And you can tear it to bits, burn the nasty, filthy thing?' Mrs Linde realises that the situation is serious, and Nora is about to say something momentous when she suddenly hears Torvald arriving. So she asks Mrs Linde to go into the children's room, with the dressmaking things; she agrees, but says that she 'won't leave the house till we've talked about this properly.'

At the beginning of this section Nora's nerves are frayed, but Mrs Linde's surprising (and dramatic) arrival soothes her, and her practical approach to repairing the dress brings some sense of normality to the situation. However, Mrs Linde is also very patronising towards Nora, whom she regards as trivial (Mrs Linde patiently and carefully repairing the vulgar Neapolitan outfit is a perfect image of how she views their relationship), and her presumption that Rank's motives are mixed demonstrates both her worldliness and, ironically in this case, the limits of her vision. We also see suggestions of Nora's own deeper feelings – towards the dress (and all it represents) and towards Rank – but these are not given time to come to the surface.

4.

As Mrs Linde hides in the neighbouring room, Torvald comes in from the hall and Nora goes to greet him. Torvald has noticed that someone has just left the room and asks if it was the dressmaker; Nora tells him that it was Mrs Linde, and

Torvald is pleased to hear that she's doing as he advised. He's just about to go into his office to do some work, when Nora says, 'If your squirrel asked for something, very, very nicely . . . would you do it?' She also promises that, if he did, 'Little songbird would chirp and sing in every room . . . I'd play fairies, dance in the moonlight.' As Torvald said she would at the end of Act One, Nora finally asks him to give Krogstad his job back; but he's astonished by her persistence. She explains that she's scared of Krogstad, and that he'll slander Torvald in the newspapers, as he did her father. Torvald explains that his situation is different – 'your father wasn't a respected public official. I am' – and adds that the fact that she's pleading for Krogstad's reinstatement makes it even harder for him to do it: 'If it comes out', he says, 'that the new manager changes his mind when his wife demands it . . . I'd be a laughing stock.' What's more, he says, even if he could overlook Krogstad's character, his old 'stupid friendship' with him would put him on intimate terms with an employee: 'It would make my position in the bank impossible.' Nora is shocked by this ('I can't believe you're so small-minded'), but she only succeeds in provoking Torvald into telling the maid to find a porter to deliver Krogstad's letter of dismissal. Nora is desperate ('Call her back, Torvald', she implores, 'There's still time. Oh Torvald, call her back – for me, for you, for the children . . . You don't know what it'll do to us'). Torvald interprets this as a symptom of her love for him ('I don't blame you, because it shows how much you love me'), but assures her that he'll be strong enough to carry the burden alone. She's terrified, and, seeing this, he assures her that they will share the burden 'as husband and wife'. Finally, he tells her to practice the tarantella and goes into his study.

In this section, we see Nora's behaviour become increasingly desperate, and she gets more and more determined to cajole Torvald, resorting to promises that she knows will stir him erotically – but which are also strikingly childish. We also see the way that Torvald so readily reverts to chauvinist self-confidence and his position in society. His powerful sense of superiority towards Krogstad – who was, he says, a friend of his – and the importance he attaches to maintaining his position provoke Nora's strongest

challenge to his authority to date. His decision to send the letter to
Krogstad is driven by pique as much as by judgment. His interpre-
tation of Nora's actions as an expression of her love for him is
brilliantly ironic: the fact is that her actions hitherto have *been*
motivated by love, but she's now clinging on for her own survival
and that of her children. Her attitude towards Torvald is chang-
ing, for the first time, but forever.

5.

Torvald leaves and 'Nora stands rooted, terrified and unsure':
'He was ready to do it', she mutters to herself, 'He can. He
will. Nothing can stop him. No. He mustn't. But how? What?'
The doorbell rings and she goes into the hall, where Rank is
hanging up his coat. She says that she recognised his ring, and
that Torvald is busy. But Rank wants to see her, not her
husband, and so she ushers him into the room and shuts the
door, telling him that she's always got time for him. But something about his tone of voice strikes her as strange, as if he
were expecting something to happen; and so, sitting beside her
by the stove, Rank makes it clear that his life is over:

> No point lying to oneself, Mrs Helmer. I'm in the worst
> state of all my patients. I've spent the last few days
> reviewing my own case. Terminal. In a month I'll be rotting
> in the churchyard.

This appals Nora, but he assures her that it is true, and adds
that as soon as he knows the worst he'll send her a visiting
card, marked with a cross, so that she'll know that 'the
dissolution, the vileness, has begun'. Nora wanted Rank to be
in 'a good mood', but he says that he cannot be, and that he's
paying the price for someone else's guilt: 'My father indulged
himself', he says, 'my poor blameless spine has to pay the bill.'
Almost hysterically, they agree on the delicious, sinful things
he's indulged in during his life – foie gras, asparagus, truffle,
oysters, port and champagne – and catch each other secretly
smiling and laughing. This prompts Nora to place both hands
on Rank's shoulders and beg him not to die, 'for Torvald, for
me'. Rank dismisses this, saying they will find someone else,
Mrs Linde for example: 'She'll take my place. When I'm dead

and done for, she'll be the one.' In reply, Nora sits on the sofa
and invites him to sit next to her, and shows him the silk
stockings that she'll wear during the tarantella, flirtatiously
asking him if he thinks they will fit, flicking his ear with them,
and deflecting his further questions ('What other delights am
I to see?' he asks). After a short pause, he speaks of his
feelings:

> When I sit here with you, so friendly, I can't . . . It's hard
> to . . . What would my life have been like if I'd never
> known this house? . . . To have to leave it forever . . .
> without a single token of what it's meant to me . . . hardly
> a backward glance . . . just an empty space for the next
> person, anyone, to fill.

This prompts Nora to ask for 'a token of friendship', and
Rank says he'd be delighted to give his help, 'the bigger the
better'. But Nora wants him to help prevent the inevitable
from happening, adding that 'Torvald loves me . . . deeply,
beyond words . . . he'd give his life'. This prompts Rank to say
that Torvald isn't the only one who would give his life for her.
At which point, she gets up, 'calmly and evenly', and calls for
Helene to bring in the lamps.

*Throughout this scene the light is slowly fading and the room
should be really quite dark by the end. The atmosphere should be
erotically charged, but never explicitly sexual, and the two of them
should share the sofa with a familiar intimacy that would have
been regarded as compromising for a bachelor and a married woman.
During the scene we see the way that Nora uses her erotic appeal
to charm Rank and manipulate him. But it also shows how terrified she is of the consequences of these actions, above all Rank's
declaration of his own feelings for her. The scene also allows us to
see Rank's darker side, particularly his scientific – and philosophical – stoicism in the face of his own imminent death.*

6.

Standing by the stove, Nora reprimands Rank for being so
bold: 'Doctor, dear Doctor, that was uncalled for.' When he
protests, she explains that what was unnecessary was telling

her. As the maid brings in the lamps, Rank realises to his amazement that she knew about his feelings for her. And so he urges her to tell him what help she needs. But, sitting on the rocking chair and smiling, she mocks him: 'Doctor, what a man you are! Aren't you embarrassed now, in proper light?' He's still perplexed, however, and declares: 'I don't understand you. I've often thought that you enjoy my company almost as much as Torvald's'. She explains that there is a distinction between enjoying people's company and loving them, and hints that although Torvald has taken her father's place in her heart, there are plenty of other people who are more fun to be with. Suddenly the maid comes in with a visiting card, which Nora glances at and quickly pockets. Rank notices that 'something's wrong', but she tells him that someone has come to see her about her fancy dress and persuades him to go into Torvald's study and keep him there, implying that it's the dress that was the big secret. He leaves obligingly, saying: 'Don't worry. He won't get away.'

The action of the maid bringing in the lamps can be made highly dramatic. Each lamp needs to be brought in already lit, set in its appropriate place, and the wick carefully turned up. This will require two journeys and a fair amount of fussing – during which time neither Rank nor Nora are able to say a word. It is only when the maid has finally left that the conversation can continue; but now the atmosphere is different – respectable, brightly lit, sober – and the erotic frisson has evaporated, replaced by Nora's mocking distance.

The moment when Nora is handed Krogstad's visiting card (carried in by the maid on a silver tray) should have a powerful dramatic impact, and her ushering of Rank into Torvald's study should negate the impression of intimacy that was so much the character of the rest of the scene.

7.

As soon as Rank has gone, Nora asks the maid if 'he [Krogstad] is in the kitchen? Waiting?' The maid tells her that he came to the back door, didn't believe her protestations that no one was in, and insisted that he had to talk to Nora. So Nora asks

Helene to bring him in 'quietly', saying that 'it's a surprise for my husband.' Left for a moment alone, Nora declares, 'It's happening. I can't stop it. I can't. I can't', and locks the study door. The maid ushers Krogstad in: 'he is wearing boots and a fur coat and cap.' He ignores Nora's requests to keep his voice down and asks her to explain why, if her husband cares so much about her, he's doing so little to save her. He realises, however, that she's said nothing to Torvald and says that he's concerned about her; he adds that it can be settled easily, 'amicably. No one has to know but the three of us'. However, she's adamant that her husband must not find out; and he says that however much she pays, he's not going to give up the document, and hints that if she had 'any crazy ideas . . . of running away' (a suggestion that she 'tonelessly' denies) the evidence would follow her. Krogstad adds that such an action would be stupid: he's written a letter to Torvald explaining everything and asking not simply for his job back, but for 'reinstatement – in a higher position' and predicts that in 'one year – less – I'll be the Manager's right hand.' When she says that this is impossible, and that she's 'brave enough now', he mocks her and tries to frighten her:

> A fine lady, airs and graces – . . . Under the ice, perhaps? In the deep, dark depths? Floating up in the spring, bloated, unrecognisable, your hair fallen out.

She says that he doesn't scare her, but he replies that she doesn't scare him either; after all, he asserts, 'no one does things like that.' What's more, he says, even if she did kill herself:

> I'd still have him [Torvald] just where I wanted him . . . Have you forgotten? I own your reputation . . . Don't do anything stupid. Helmer will get my letter. I'll wait for a reply. And remember this: it was him, your husband, who forced me to do this. I'll never forgive him for that.

And out he goes through the hall. Nora stands at the door, holds it open and listens. For a moment she thinks he's not going to leave the letter in the box. There is a pause, in which she can sense that Krogstad is standing outside the door, not going downstairs. She's just about to convince herself that he's changed his mind when the 'letter falls into the box and we hear Krogstad's steps dying away as he goes down the stairs'. 'With a stifled shriek', Nora crosses to the table by the sofa and realises what has happened. She creeps back to the hall door and laments.

The fact that Krogstad has come in through the back door, and plays the scene in his coat and hat, emphasises that he's from the outside and has found his way into the very heart of Nora's life. It also makes it clear that this is a visit that he wants to keep secret. Nora is aware that the momentum is building and that the disaster is becoming inevitable. It is important that Krogstad's protestations of concern for Nora should sound genuine; but we should also see his utter determination to regain respectability and status. Krogstad's empathy with Nora is the understanding of a fellow criminal, and he knows that she'll consider running away, even killing herself. We should regard his prediction of her cowardice as an underestimation, but be shocked by his claim of posthumous power over her reputation. It is important to realise that in Nora's mind the catastrophe that's approaching is one that she'll be sharing with her husband: 'Torvald, oh Torvald, he's finished us.'

The final section, above all Krogstad's lingering at the door before he drops the letter in the locked box, is deliberately dramatic. It also suggests that he's genuinely struggling with his conscience and aware of the destructive power of what he's doing. His decision has more impact because of his initial hesitancy.

8.

Mrs Linde comes back in, with the fancy dress that she's now repaired, and asks Nora if she wants to try it on. But Nora is deeply disturbed ('what's the matter?' asks Mrs Linde, 'You look terrified') and shows her the letter lying in the locked box. Mrs Linde insists that it is best for both of them that Torvald should find out what has happened, but is shocked when Nora confesses that she forged a signature. Nora insists that she, Mrs Linde, should speak for her if she had to go away and someone else tried to take the blame. When Mrs Linde says that she doesn't understand, Nora's answer is cryptic: 'Why should you understand? What's going to happen . . . is a miracle!'

Suddenly, to Nora's astonishment, Mrs Linde announces that she'll visit Krogstad, explaining that 'Once, he'd have done anything for my sake'. She's fishing for his visiting card in her pocket when Torvald knocks on the door of his study, calling out Nora's name. Because the door is locked, he's convinced that she must be trying out her new dress. Nora assures him that she'll be 'so pretty'; but tells Mrs Linde, 'It's too late. We're finished. The letter's in the box. There in the hall.' Mrs Linde races off, determined to persuade Krogstad to ask for his letter back, unopened.

The return of Mrs Linde brings a sense of normality back into the scene: if only Nora's marriage could be as easily mended as the fancy dress. Mrs Linde's insistence that Nora and Torvald should face up to the truth is both admirable and naïve, as her astonishment at the details shows. It is now that Nora first talks of the 'miracle', a phrase she uses to describe the only two available possibilities: either Torvald will understand what has happened and take on the responsibility for it, or something even more radical will happen that will transform everything – namely, her own death by suicide. The strange thing is that Nora herself doesn't know what shape the miracle will take: both transformation and suicide seem impossible but the final outcome, leaving the marriage, has not yet dawned on her.

Nora is also amazed by Mrs Linde's determination to visit Krogstad to persuade him to behave differently; she too has a limited knowledge of the facts. The scene ends with Nora certain of imminent disaster, and Mrs Linde working hard to avoid it. The audience should be left unsure about who is going to be right.

9.

As soon as Mrs Linde has gone, 'Nora goes to Helmer's study, opens the door and peeps in'. We can hear Torvald offstage inviting Rank to come and see Nora's 'transformation'. But Nora answers that 'No one's to admire my dress till tomorrow morning'. Seeing how tired she looks, he wonders if she's been practising too hard; Nora, however, says that she needs his help, and that she's 'terrified [of] all those people.' Torvald promises that he will, but first he has to see if the post has arrived. Nora pleads with him, telling him that there isn't any, and when he sets off for the hall regardless she 'runs to the piano and plays the first few bars of the tarantella'. This stops Torvald, who is genuinely surprised ('You're really nervous?' he asks), and she begs him to play the piano for her: 'Play, and watch, and put me right.' He sits down at the piano while she takes a tambourine and a long shawl out of the box, 'jumps centre front and cries "I'm ready! Play!"' Torvald tries to control the pace, saying 'slower, slower', but Nora is unstoppable. Rank offers to play instead, and Nora dances, ever more wildly. Meanwhile, Torvald:

> has taken his place by the stove, and directs her as she dances. She seems not to hear him. Her hair falls over her shoulders, and she pays no attention. She is engrossed in the dance.

As Nora's crisis intensifies, Torvald becomes increasingly complacent; the contrast between them is deliberately pronounced. Of course, Torvald is encouraged in this by Nora's persistent and increasing play-acting. This reaches a climax with her desperate dancing of the tarantella. Torvald finds this peculiar but humours her nonetheless. The overall sensation at the end of the act should be of a sudden acceleration of tempo and emotion, which drives all before it.

The tarantella itself is a very particular kind of dance. It is essential that it should show an escalating sense of catastrophe, and express Nora's growing – and almost fatalistic – struggle with her situation. It's as if she hopes dancing the tarantella will rid her of the poison that's killing her.

The tarantella needs to be seen in its dramatic context: Nora is ostensibly practising for the fancy dress party, but more immediately is distracting Torvald from the letter box. The danger with the tarantella in the theatre is that it is sometimes turned into something bigger than it is, almost a song-and-dance routine in the middle of the play, with no credibility at all. One way of preventing this is for Nora to dance frantically but inexpertly.

10.

Suddenly, in the midst of all this, Mrs Linde returns, and 'stands at the door amazed'. As she dances, Nora calls to her ('Look, Kristine, look!), and Torvald says: 'Nora, darling, any-one'd think your life depended on this dance'; her reply is, 'It does.' Torvald tells Rank to stop playing the piano, and 'Nora suddenly stands still'. Torvald reprimands her ('You've for-gotten the whole thing') and tells her that she needs to practise. She agrees: 'Today, tomorrow, concentrate on me. Nothing else. No letters. Don't even open the post box.' He's aston-ished ('you're still afraid of him') and wonders whether Krogstad has written a letter. But Nora is persistent: 'But don't read it. Not now. Nothing nasty must come between us, not now, not now.' Encouraged by Rank ('Better humour her'), Torvald concurs: 'Whatever my darling wants.' When he adds 'But tomorrow night, when you've done your dancing . . .' her reply is an ominous: 'Then you're free.'

The arrival of Mrs Linde brings a new intensity to a scene that's already highly charged. She provides Nora with a bigger audience, but watches the increasingly frenetic dance with objectivity and informed astonishment. The contrast with Torvald – who only sees the surface, Nora practising her dance for the party – is telling. When Nora is made to stop by Torvald, she sees that even her most extreme attempts at distraction are unsuccessful, and so resorts to a direct appeal. It's at this point that Torvald notices that something is wrong, but again fails to grasp the extent of her desperation. It's with almost resigned amazement that Torvald agrees to her pleas; her final reply is a prediction which is truer than either of them can imagine.

11.

Helene, the maid, comes in to announce that dinner is served, and, to Torvald's astonishment, Nora calls for champagne: 'A banquet, all night long. Champagne! And macaroons, Helene. Platefuls of macaroons.' Torvald tries to calm her down ('Sh, sh. Little singing bird, there, there'), but she ushers the men into the dining room and asks Mrs Linde to help her put her hair up. As they go, Rank asks Torvald obliquely if she's pregnant, which Torvald quickly denies ('No, no, no. My dear fellow! Over-excited, that's all').

Nora's extravagance partly derives from a kind of devil-may-care chutzpah *brought on by the tarantella, but more from her growing sense that she's at the brink of disaster. Rank's coded inquiry about Nora's possible pregnancy reflects contemporary medical views on the womb as the seat of 'hysteria',* [18] *and strikes him as the most obvious cause; Torvald's instant denial suggests that their sexual relations are non-existent.*

12.

Left alone together, Mrs Linde tells Nora that Krogstad has left town and will be 'back tomorrow afternoon', but that she's left him a note. Nora wishes she had not done so and says: 'You can't stop it. A miracle's going to happen, and we're celebrating.' Mrs Linde goes off to join the men for dinner, and Nora gathers her thoughts:

> Five o'clock. Seven hours till midnight. Then twenty-four hours till tomorrow midnight. Twenty-four and seven. Thirty-one. Thirty-one hours left, to live.

Finally, Torvald comes back and asks 'What's keeping my little singing bird?' She runs to him with open arms, declaring 'Here she is! Here!'

Once the men leave, the atmosphere changes immediately and the women get to the point. Nora speaks again of the 'miracle' that she's convinced must take place. At this point, she's conceiving of something very different from the eventual outcome and it's becoming clear to her that the miracle will only be achieved through suicide. Indeed, one could say that Nora's increasingly frantic concern with the nature of this miracle is the main drama of the third, and final, act, of the play.

Act Three

Act Three takes place late at night on Boxing Day. 'The table and chairs have been moved centre and there is a lighted lamp on the table.'

The atmosphere of this last act is very different from the first two. It is late at night, and it's very cold outside. Furthermore, the Christmas celebrations are effectively over. The room should feel like a place of shadows, overheated and claustrophobic, a zone for adults with the children safely asleep; but it's also where new futures can be negotiated. The lamp on the table provides the bright centre to the room; it should be the main source of light and acts as a metaphor for the illumination which will dawn on all the characters before the end of the play.

I.

Ibsen's stage directions are precise: 'The hall door is open and dance-music can be heard from the upstairs apartment. Mrs Linde is sitting at the table turning the pages of a book. She's trying to read but finds it hard to concentrate.' She glances at her watch in anticipation, but is concerned that 'he' won't turn up. Suddenly she hears a sound and 'carefully opens the main door. Light steps can be heard on the stairs outside'. She whispers to someone to come in, saying, 'There's no one here.'

The sound of the dance music coming from upstairs should be muffled but convey a slightly hysterical atmosphere. It's possible that the audience should be able to hear laughter and other party sounds overhead – even the thudding of dancing, but not yet the tarantella.

By contrast, Mrs Linde is entirely isolated, completely sober and nervous about Krogstad's arrival. She's like a young girl waiting for her lover; but she's also a mature woman who knows that her prospects of future happiness depend on the outcome of this meeting.

2.

Krogstad arrives, saying that Mrs Linde had left a note for
him to come. When she tells him that the Helmers are upstairs
at a party, he's surprised but won't say why. He rebuffs her
attempts to talk, describing her as 'a heartless woman' who
jilted him as soon as a better chance came along. But she
defends herself, saying that he, Krogstad, had no prospects
then, and that she had a sick mother and two young brothers
to look after. This doesn't reassure him: 'When I lost you, it
was like being shipwrecked.' She says she 'had no idea it was
your job they were giving me' and that they should help each
other like 'two drowning people', adding, 'All my life, as long
as I can remember, I've worked. It's been my greatest pleasure,
my only pleasure. Now I'm alone . . . empty, thrown away.
Where's the satisfaction in working for oneself? Nils, give me
someone, something to work for.' Krogstad's first reaction is to
reject this ('Hysteria', he says. 'Female hysteria. Extravagant
self-sacrifice, that's what this is.') but he quickly realises that
she's utterly serious and will accept him for what he is: 'I need
someone to mother', she says. 'Your children need a mother;
you and I need each other. I trust you, Nils, the man you really
are.' He takes her hands and thanks her, saying that now he
can 'climb again'. But hearing the sound of the tarantella
being danced upstairs, he remembers what he's done to the
Helmers. They both look at the letter in the box, and he suddenly becomes suspicious of her motives: 'It's her you want to
save', he cries. She reassures him and, when he says that he'll
ask for the letter back, she says, to his amazement, that 'Helmer
must know the truth. The secret must come out. No more lies,
tricks, they must understand each other.' She hurries him out
and he declares: 'This is the luckiest day of my life.'

*The relationship between Mrs Linde and Krogstad acts as a
powerful counterpoint to that of Nora and Torvald: whereas they
go from apparent marital bliss to painful separation, Mrs Linde
and Krogstad find happiness and redemption with each other.
Ibsen's psychological sophistication understands the depth of Krogstad's hurt and his innate suspicion of the woman who inflicted it.
Mrs Linde combines tremendous courage and independence with a
deeply-rooted desire to work for others, to have a purpose in life as*

a helper and homemaker. Thus their reconciliation is in no sense sentimental or improbable.

One of the most startling moments is Mrs Linde's insistence that Nora and Torvald should face up to the reality of their situation. It reflects Ibsen's own concern in the play that self-realisation is only possible when the truth has been grasped. It's important, however, to realise that Mrs Linde's action leads to pain as well as rebirth, and that such a decision shouldn't be taken lightly.

3.

After Krogstad's departure there is a short pause in which Mrs Linde tidies up the room, fetches her coat and says to herself: 'At last. Someone to work for, live for. A home.' Soon, Nora and Torvald are outside, and we hear his key in the door. He then 'all but drags Nora into the hall'; she can be heard protesting that she wants to go back upstairs – 'Please, Torvald. Please. Another hour. For little Nora. Please.' – but Torvald insists and leads her in.

This small section allows us to glimpse something of Torvald and Nora's relationship. Nora doesn't want to come downstairs, mainly because she knows what he'll find in the letter box, but Torvald has become aroused by the sight of Nora dancing the tarantella and wants to get her into bed. It's also clear that he's been drinking and here it's important to remember the role of alcohol in nineteenth-century Scandinavia: namely, it was largely frowned on, except in particular social circumstances when it was common to drink in large quantities. Thus the fancy dress party has been an 'adults only' event – an echo of the Roman midwinter feast of excess, the Saturnalia – and very unlike the usual run of things.

Throughout all this, of course, Mrs Linde is standing in the living room, perhaps in the dark. It's intriguing to imagine what she's feeling: possibly she takes it as further evidence of the superficiality – and precariousness – of Torvald and Nora's relationship.

4.

Nora and Torvald enter: 'She is wearing the Italian dress and a large black shawl; he is in evening dress, with a black, swirling cloak.' They're surprised to see Mrs Linde; but when she explains that she wanted to see Nora in her dress, Torvald takes the shawl off her and presents his wife: 'Isn't she pretty? Isn't she delightful?' he boasts. He then describes what happened upstairs; how she danced her tarantella ('a little more . . . energetic than artistic') but was reluctant to come downstairs again. In language that's richly erotic, he describes what happened next:

> Was I going to let her stay after that? Spoil the effect? Of course I wasn't. I took my little Capri fishergirl – my delicious, capricious little fishergirl – on my arm . . . swift tour round the room, curtsey here, curtsey there – and the vision of loveliness was gone, as they say in fairy tales.

Torvald throws his cloak over a chair and goes into the study to light a couple of candles. Nora asks Mrs Linde what has happened. She tells her that she talked to Krogstad and that she, Nora, must tell Torvald everything. Nora is terrified, but Mrs Linde assures her that Krogstad won't hurt her. Torvald returns and asks Mrs Linde if she's gazed her fill. When she announces that she'll say goodnight, Torvald hands her her knitting, and tells her that she should take up embroidery instead, declaring that it's 'far more becoming'. Torvald has drunk more than usual ('That was wonderful champagne') and doesn't offer to see Mrs Linde home; when she leaves, he calls her a 'boring woman'.

This is the first time that we have seen Nora in her Neapolitan costume and the visual effect should be startling. It should bring a new range of colours on the stage: yellows and reds, garish tassels and decorations. It should also introduce overt eroticism, albeit of a somewhat humiliating kind. Torvald's evening suit and his black swirling cloak also add to the change in atmosphere. Fuelled by champagne, he has a new kind of masculine pride – which verges on the boorish – and enjoys showing off his wife; he's also less formal in his behaviour towards Mrs Linde and is keen for her to leave. As soon as he's offstage, however, we see the opposite: Nora's deep anxiety about Krogstad and Mrs Linde's sober insistence that she should tell her husband the truth.

5.

Left alone together, Nora asks Torvald if he's tired; on the contrary, he declares, he's 'wide awake, full of beans', but adds that *she* looks tired and kisses her forehead, saying: 'You see! I was right, to make you come away.' Torvald is pleased to be alone with her, and speaks of his erotic feelings for her:

> Aha! Little Tarantella still? More delicious than ever. Listen! The guests are leaving. Nora, soon it'll be so still, so still . . . Darling, you know when I'm out with you, at a party, when I hardly talk to you, just glance at you now and then – d'you know why I do that? I'm pretending we're secret lovers, that we're promised to one another, and it's our secret, no one knows but us . . . When it's time to come away, and I'm arranging the shawl on your pretty shoulders, your lovely neck, I imagine you're my new young bride, we've just come back from the wedding, I'm bringing you home for the very first time . . . we're alone for the very first time . . . alone, my shy little, sweet little darling. All evening I've longed for nothing else but you. When I saw you twirling, swirling in the tarantella, my blood pounded, I couldn't bear it, I hurried you, hurried you down here –

But making love is the last thing she wants; and she tells him to let go of her. Suddenly there is a knock at the outer door.

In this scene, we should see how the champagne has loosened Torvald's inhibitions, and released the strength of his erotic feelings for Nora. We should also see her revulsion at his advances, and notice that she shrinks away. Although this should be expressed in physical action, it's a mistake to imagine it staged in such a way that he's using his strength to sexually possess her. Although her appeal is almost pornographic – her fancy dress is tight fitting and garish, and she may well be wearing more makeup than usual – the scene does not contain sexual violence; rather, released by champagne and the memory of the tarantella that she's just danced, Torvald's arousal is revealing and almost tender. The scene should show the depth of misunderstanding that has arisen between them, rather than pour scorn on his sexual feelings. The point is that it's

only in the 'true marriage' that Nora talks about later – a mar-
riage based on truth and equality, rather than the fantasy Torvald
has been indulging in – that Torvald's sexuality can be given the
place it deserves, and be reciprocated.

6.

Both Nora and Torvald are startled to hear Rank's voice asking to come in; indeed, Torvald is rather put out by it, but he
opens the door and welcomes him in. Rank has enjoyed
himself – Torvald says earlier that he's hardly ever seen him
so happy – and now he wants to see 'These dear, familiar
rooms. Such a happy, cosy home'. When Torvald points out
that he obviously enjoyed the party, Rank's answer is, 'Why
shouldn't I? Why shouldn't we enjoy every blessed thing? As
much as we can, as long as we can', adding that he was amazed
how much he managed to 'put away: a jolly evening after a
well spent day.' Nora adds that Torvald drank a great deal too
('It goes straight to his head') and asks Rank whether his day
was spent in 'Scientific work . . . [an] investigation?' He confirms that it was and that the result is 'final – for both the
doctor and the patient' – and they agree that he deserved a
'jolly evening'. 'At next year's fancy dress party', he says, she'll
go as 'a good-luck pixie' – dressed in 'her ordinary clothes' –
and he'll be 'invisible', wearing 'a big black hat'. Rank asks
Torvald for a cigar, 'one of the dark Havanas'; Torvald offers
him the case, and Nora lights one for him. He says goodbye
and leaves: 'Sleep well', he says, 'and thanks for the light.'

Rank's surprise visit acts as an important transition in the climac-
tic third act. He should be dressed in a dinner suit – an especially
expensive one – and behave as if he's drunk a great deal of
champagne. However, he's as friendly and flirtatious as ever,
charming and resolutely dedicated to the pursuit of sensual
pleasure. He is also – as we'll shortly discover – convinced of the
imminence of his death and knows that this will be his last visit to
the Helmers, a couple to whom he has, in different ways, been very
close. Much of what he says is in code, which only Nora can
understand, and makes Torvald feel uncomfortable. His joke that
at next year's fancy dress party he'll be 'invisible' is one of the
most chilling moments in the play. Nora's lighting of Rank's cigar

is one of the most erotic; but it's also as if she were lighting his way to his death.

7.

With Rank's departure, Torvald's mood changes rapidly; he takes his keys out of his pocket and goes into the hall to empty the letter box. There he discovers that someone has been tampering with the lock, and discovers a broken hairpin. He gruffly accepts her explanation that it must have been one of the children and calls out towards the kitchen, telling Helene to extinguish the front door lamp. He comes back with a stack of letters and notices two of Rank's visiting cards. Above the printed name – 'Lars Johan Rank, Bachelor of Medicine' – there is a black cross in ink: 'You'd think he was announcing his own death', says Torvald. Nora confirms that this is the case and that Rank had said that once he'd delivered his visiting card, he'd lock himself in, to die. Torvald is mortified:

> My friend. My poor friend. I knew we wouldn't have him long. But so soon, and shutting himself away like a wounded animal . . . He was like family. I can't imagine him . . . gone. Unhappy, lonely – he was like the sky, and our happiness was the Sun.

He consoles himself, however, with the notion that Rank's death might be good for their marriage and, putting his arms around her, says:

> We've no one else now, just each other. Darling wife, I can never hold you tight enough. D'you know, I've often wished you were in some deadly danger, so that I could give my heart's blood, my life, for you.

She, however, firmly disengages herself and tells him to open the letters. He protests ('I want to be with you, darling. With my wife'), but she tells him to think of Rank. He agrees and says that they should sleep in separate rooms. She throws her arms around him, and he kisses her on the forehead ('Sleep well, little songbird') and walks into his study to read the letters.

*With the discovery of Rank's marked visiting cards, death finally
enters the play. Rank has provided the glue for their marriage –
acting as Nora's confidant and Torvald's advisor – and his
imminent death leaves a hole that both of them feel. It demonstrates to her the transience of all things and the proximity of death
as the ultimate escape from troubles; it throws him onto his own,
somewhat limited resources, both in terms of his marriage and the
world outside. Torvald's determination to extract a positive from
the situation shows his innate optimism, as well as his ignorance
that the time has come to face up to the truth. It also reveals his
ambivalence towards the death of a man who flirts so blatantly
with his wife.*

*There is a fascinating psychological reversal in this section. Nora
is now insisting that Torvald should read the very letter that at the
beginning of the act scared her so much. Of course, it must be
understood that Nora's impulse here is in many ways negative:
she's decided that the time has come to provoke the catastrophe
that's now as inevitable as Rank's death.*

8.

For the first time in the act, Nora is left alone. Wild-eyed, she
fumbles around, takes Torvald's big black cloak and throws it
round her shoulders. In a hoarse, broken whisper she says:
'Never again. Never see him again.' She then pulls the shawl
over her head and contemplates the reality of losing her children. Delirious, she talks of 'the water . . . deep . . . black.' She
realises that 'He's opened it. He's reading it' and mutters a
good-bye to Torvald and her 'little ones'. She's just about to
hurry out through the hall when Torvald opens the study door
and stands there, with an open letter in his hands.

*This is the lowest moment in the entire play for Nora, and when
she comes closest to running out of the door and throwing herself
into the sea. Ibsen's stage direction suggests that she should wrap
the black cloak all round her and the visual effect is extraordinarily
powerful: it hides the gaudy Neapolitan fancy dress entirely and
provides a theatrical metaphor for the disappearance that she's
considering. The despair that she reaches here is the opposite of the
new life that she is ultimately given.*

9.

Nora is shocked by Torvald's appearance and screams. When he asks her if she knows what the letter says, she admits that she does and tries to leave. Torvald stops her and asks: 'It's true? What he writes, it's true? Unbearable. It's not, it can't be.' She protests – 'You were more than all the world to me' – but Torvald insists that she has to face up to the facts. When he asks if she understands what she's done, she looks directly at him, and for the first time the 'frost forms in her voice': '*Now* I understand', she says. This doesn't stop Torvald from pacing up and down, berating her and feeling sorry for himself:

> I should have expected it. I should have known. Like father
> – sh! – like daughter. No religion, no ethics, no sense of
> duty. I shut my eyes to what he was like – for your sake, for
> you – and this is what I get. This is how you repay me . . .
> You've killed my happiness. You've destroyed my future.
> I'm trapped, in his [Krogstad's] claws. No mercy. He'll do
> whatever he likes to me, demand, insist, I can't refuse. No
> way out. A silly, empty-headed woman – and now I'm dead.

Incapable of hearing her increasingly chilly protestations that once she's out of the way he'll be free, he's particularly struck when he realises that people will think that it was his idea and that he was behind it all. Nevertheless, he tries to get a grip and declares that 'It *must* be hushed up', that they must go on as if nothing had changed between them. But he adds a final sting:

> But I won't have you near the children. I can never trust
> you again. Fancy having to say that to you – the woman I
> loved, I still . . . No. It's gone. Happiness is gone.

Nora's reaction to Torvald's appearance is one of extreme shock. He hardly hears her brief, but all-important explanation ('You were all the world to me') and immediately blames her; it's this which turns her cold, which affects the rest of the act – and the end of their marriage. It's in this section that Nora first sees just how egocentric Torvald is, and understands how limited his notion of

*love is. Her intention is still suicidal, but as he talks she sees him
for what he is: self-centred, judgmental and, ultimately, hypo-
critical.*

10.

Suddenly the doorbell rings. For a moment Torvald is terrified that it is Krogstad and tells Nora to hide, but she stands
motionless as he unlocks the hall door. The maid is standing
in her nightclothes, with a letter 'for madam'. He takes the
letter, shuts the door and moves over to the lamp to read it. He
pauses a moment ('It could be the end of both of us'), but then
'tears open the letter, reads a few lines, and shouts with joy'.
Checking it again, he tells her that he's saved, that both of
them are saved; he tells her that Krogstad says he's sorry and
that his life has changed. He then tears up the contract which
Krogstad had enclosed and both letters and stuffs them into
the stove, instructing her to 'shout for joy'. Surprised to see
her 'icy face', he assures her that he's forgiven her everything:

> You loved me as all wives should love their husbands. You
> were new to it, that's all; you didn't understand what you
> were doing. But don't think I love you any less, just because
> you don't know how to manage things. I'll guide you, darling,
> I'll protect you. Lean on me. I'd hardly be a man if feminine
> weakness, your weakness, didn't make me love you even
> more. These hard words, when I thought everything was
> lost – forget them. I've forgiven you, Nora. I swear I've
> forgiven you.

Her response is a sardonic 'You're very kind'.

*The sound of the doorbell is the very last thing either Torvald or
Nora expects; Ibsen has created a deliberately dramatic pause, in
which he panics and she's defiant. They both think the hour of
truth – their nemesis – has arrived, and the sight of the maid in her
nightclothes with a letter in her hand should be bathetic. The stage
direction indicating a move over to the lamp suggests just how dark
the rest of the room should be, and Ibsen asks for another pause in
which Torvald hesitates to read the letter. Torvald's reaction is one*

of unbridled joy – like a child let off homework – and his burning of the letters and the contract demonstrates his desperate desire for the whole unhappy episode to be covered up. And, of course, having narrowly escaped disaster, he's full of Christian forgiveness and manly strength. This episode is dangerously prone to laughter from a modern audience; while Ibsen's intentions are as ironic as Nora's reply, it would be a grave mistake for the actor playing Torvald to 'play for laughs' here. Throughout, we should see Nora's position gradually hardening.

Although Krogstad doesn't appear in this section it's important that the actor – and the audience – has been led to understand at the beginning of the act both his desire to be a reformed and respectable character, and Mrs Linde's influence over him. Otherwise, this second letter can appear like an unrealistic deus ex machina.

11.

Nora suddenly leaves the room, to change. While she's offstage, Torvald paces up and down talking to her through an open door:

> Be calm, be calm, my frightened little bird. Nothing will hurt you; I'll spread my wings, I'll shelter you. It's warm and cosy, our nest, our home. Nothing will hurt you. Poor frightened dove, I'll save you from the hawk, I'll keep you safe. Still, little fluttering heart, be still. It'll be all right. Darling, you'll see.

But he's amazed to discover that she's not changed into her nightclothes, but into ordinary day clothes. She asks him to sit down at the table where, she says, 'we have to come to terms'.

Nora's decision to leave the marriage occurs moments before she goes to change her clothes, but it has grown in response to Torvald's reactions, to Krogstad's revelation, then to his letter of reprieve. It's important that she leaves the door open as she changes (perhaps a bright light should stream out of that room into the dark drawing room). Although Torvald's speech is intended for her ears, much of what he's saying is for his own benefit, as a way of reassuring himself that all is as it should be. He imagines her changing into her nightclothes, and it's quite possible that he now wants the evening to end, after all, in lovemaking. He should be utterly astonished when she comes back in a sober dress for going out – which should contrast as much as possible with the garish costume – and even more surprised when she asks him to sit down on the other side of the table, as if he was attending a business meeting.

12.

Sitting face to face across the table, Nora tells Torvald that 'there's a lot to say'. When he says that he doesn't understand, her reply is: 'Exactly. You don't understand me. And I've never understood you – until just now. Don't say anything. Listen. It's time to come to terms.' She tells him that it's strange that in their eight years of marriage, this is the first time they have sat down together to talk seriously. She feels that he and her father before him have done her 'great wrong': 'You never loved me', she says. 'Either of you. It pleased you, that's all – the idea of loving me.' Her father told her his views on everything, and she had to agree with them; if she didn't, she says, 'he called me his little dolly-baby, and played with me as I played with my dollies.' When she married Torvald, exactly the same thing happened: 'I've existed to perform for you, Torvald', she tells him. 'That's what you wanted. You've done me great harm, you and Daddy: you've blocked my life.' Astonished by this, he asks, 'Haven't you been happy here?' But her reply is to the point:

> No, never. I thought I was, but I wasn't. [I was] cheerful. You've always been kind to me. But it's as if we live in a Wendy house. I'm your dolly-wife, just as I used to be Daddy's dolly-baby. And my dolls were the children. When you played with me, I had a lovely time – and so did they when I played with them. That's our marriage, Torvald. That's what it's been like.

Torvald accepts this – 'Maybe you're right. Hysterical, over-wrought, but a little bit right' – but adds, 'Now things are going to change. Playtime ends; lessons begin'. Nora knows that what he's talking about is him doing the teaching, and declares that he couldn't teach her to be a proper wife, nor, as he said so himself, can she teach the children anymore. And then she announces that she's leaving him.

It's only once she's sitting facing her husband across the table that Nora is able, finally, to say the things that have been building up over the years, and that have been brought to a head in the last few minutes. Significantly, she looks back over her entire life, not just her marriage, and tells Torvald that the pattern of her relationship with him was set in the way that her father treated her when she was young. Her central complaint is that she's been infantilised by the two most important men in her life and that this has damaged her capacity for growth and achievement. Torvald is concerned about her, but his solution – to be her teacher – simply continues the father-daughter relationship that she needs to break.

13.

Torvald is amazed to hear Nora say that she's leaving. But she's deadly serious:

> If I'm to come to terms with myself, understand myself, I have to be alone. I can't stay here . . . I'll go right away. I'll sleep at Kristine's tonight.

When he says that he 'forbids' her to leave, she snaps back ('No more forbidding') and tells him that tomorrow she'll go home: 'I mean where I was born. I'll find something there.' Torvald cannot believe that she'll risk what people will say and reminds her of her 'most sacred obligations'. But she says she has 'other obligations, just as sacred . . . To myself':

> I think that first I'm a human being, the same as you. Or at least that I'll try to be one. I know that most people would agree with you, Torvald, that's what they teach in books. But I've had enough of what most people say, what they write in books. It's not enough. I must think things out for myself, I must decide.

When Torvald asks her if she has no beliefs to guide her, she replies that Pastor Hansen used to tell her what to think, but now she needs to work it out for herself. Undeterred, Torvald asks whether she has a conscience, any sense of morality. Her answer goes to the heart of the reason she's leaving:

I can't answer. I don't know. I'm baffled. All I know is, you
and I have different ideas about it all. And the law – I've
discovered that's not what I always thought it was, and I
can't believe it's right. A woman mustn't spare her dying
father, or save her husband's life. I can't believe it.

When he pours scorn on this ('You're talking like a child. You
don't understand the society you live in'), her reply is sharp
and to the point: 'You're right', she says, 'I don't. But I'm
going to find out – which of us is right, society or me.'

*Nora's almost casual announcement that she's leaving shocks
Torvald profoundly, but once again his instinct is to try to reassert
his authority and forbid her. Nora's response takes more courage,
and is more radical, than can be easily imagined today. Torvald's
second appeal is to her sense of morality, conscience, her sacred
duty; once again Nora shows that she's defying the basis for all the
value systems she's known since she was a child. It's vital that this
shouldn't be played as churlishness or sullen rebellion. In these last
minutes of the play, Nora's strength lies in her quiet, intellectual
seriousness, not in a display of histrionics or excessive emotion. It's
clear that the miracles she spoke of earlier – Torvald's conversion
or her suicide – are not going to take place, and that the real
transformation is going to take place within her: from doll's house
to adult life, from prison to freedom, from death to life.*

14.

Torvald tells her that she's ill, delirious even. But Nora says
she's never felt better and that her mind has never been
clearer. He declares that there is only one explanation – she's
stopped loving him – and she agrees. This appals him, but she
persists: 'It hurts, Torvald. You've always been wonderful to
me. But I can't help it. I've just stopped loving you . . . It's why
I'm going.' When he asks he what he did to lose her love, her
reply is mysterious:

It was tonight. The miracle didn't happen. I saw you
weren't the man I'd imagined. For eight years I've waited
patiently. Miracles don't happen every day, God knows.
Then I was engulfed in catastrophe, and I was certain: it'll
happen now, the miracle.

He's baffled, but she soon explains what she means:

> When Krogstad sent his letter, I was certain you'd never
> give in to him. You'd tell him to publish and be damned . . .
> I was certain you'd take the whole thing on your own
> shoulders, and say, 'I did it. I was the guilty one' . . . You
> think I'd have denied it? Of course I would. But what
> would my word be worth, compared with yours? That was
> the miracle I hoped for.

'No man sacrifices his *honour* for the one he loves', says
Torvald; 'Hundreds of thousand of women do just that' is her
quick reply.

*Torvald quickly resorts to abuse, but it's fuelled by hurt and
confusion. His declaration that she must have stopped loving him
is full of self-pity, and he's shocked when she confirms that this is
the case. He finds her reference to the 'miracle' mystifying, but
Nora is being deliberately ironic: in other words, she now sees that
the fact that he let her down is just the first step in her progress
towards being able to stand on her own two feet. His privileging of
his masculine honour brings the entire debate between the two into
the sharpest possible focus.*

15.

Finally, standing up from the table, Nora summarises what has
happened this evening:

> As soon as you stopped panicking – not panicking for me,
> but for what might happen to you – when it was over, you
> behaved as if nothing at all had happened. So far as you
> were concerned, I went back to what I'd always been: your
> pet bird, your doll, which you'd now have to treat with
> extra care because I was fragile, breakable. That's when I
> realised, Torvald. For eight years I've lived with a stranger.
> Borne him three children. I can't bear it. I'd like to tear
> myself to pieces.

Desperately, Torvald begs her to stay: 'I'll change. I can
change . . . Don't leave me. I don't understand.' But she's
impervious, and fetches her cloak and a small suitcase from

the next room. When he asks her to live with him as 'brother and sister', she says that it wouldn't last. So she puts on her shawl and says goodbye, adding that she doesn't want to see the children, saying 'They're in better hands than mine'. Torvald tries everything, but Nora's conclusion is clear:

> When a wife deserts her husband, as I'm deserting you, the law frees him of all obligations towards her. And in any case, I set you free. You're not bound in any way. You're free. We're both free. On both sides: freedom.

She gives him back her ring, takes his, and puts her keys on the table. Her tone is utterly practical:

> The servants know where everything is – better than I do. Tomorrow, as soon as I've left the town, Kristine will come and pack my things – my own things, the things I brought from home. I'll have them sent on.

In despair, Torvald asks if she'll ever think of him; 'often', she says, 'you, the children, this house', but forbids him to write to her or try to help her in any way: 'I'll take nothing from a stranger.' When he asks if he can ever be anything more than a stranger to her, she picks up the case and asks: 'If the miracle happened . . . If we changed, both of us, if we –' But it's impossible, she says, 'I've stopped believing in miracles'. Still Torvald presses, and she tells him that the only condition would be, 'If we discovered some true relationship'.

The moment when Nora stands up at the table changes the balance between the two: suddenly Torvald is the supplicant and Nora is the dominant one, the goddess refusing favours. From this point on she's utterly clear in her actions, and although there must be an undercurrent of pain – at leaving her husband, her house, and her children – each move should be clearly defined and executed without hesitation or possibility of confusion. Nora's disavowal of miracles is her final metamorphosis – or disillusionment, depending on your perspective – and her last reply to Torvald expresses the real, domestic, practical but world-changing truth.

16.

With a final 'Goodbye', Nora goes out through the hall.
Torvald 'slumps into a chair by the door and covers his face'
calling out her name desperately. He then gets up, looks
round and sees that the room is empty. For a moment 'a hope
flashes across his face', and he wonders about the possibility
of a miracle. But the final stage direction says it all: 'A door
slams, off.'

*By the last moments of the play Torvald should be a broken man,
and it's essential for its balance and meaning that we should set
Nora's act of transformation and self-realisation against the pain
of the husband who loved her – and whom she loved – and the
children she is leaving behind. This isn't to turn the play on its
head and argue that Ibsen's point is that she shouldn't leave; it's
that the last moments of the play should be infused by a terrible
sense of tragic necessity.*

The Characters

Fundamental to all naturalistic theatre – and Ibsen's in particular – is the presentation of fully rounded, three-dimensional characters, driven by clearly defined motives, rooted in the realities of their background and their situation, and alive with contradiction and complexity. While there is inevitably a danger in looking at fictional characters from a psychoanalytical perspective (after all, they're not real people, merely the product of the writer's imagination), it's essential that anybody trying to imagine A Doll's House *on stage should look at them carefully and try to understand what it is that makes them do what they do. One of the extraordinary things about the play – particularly after the large casts required by* Brand, Peer Gynt *and* Pillars of the Community *– is how Ibsen manages to have such a powerful effect with such a restricted* dramatis personae. *This is only possible because his characters are drawn in such detail and are so carefully balanced against each other.*

NORA

Nora Helmer is the wife of the newly-appointed bank manager, Torvald Helmer, and the mother of three young children. She's a highly intelligent, attractive, capable young woman, living in a world where her innate abilities have not been given scope to develop.

Although Ibsen doesn't specify Nora's age (he's very particular about this with other characters, such as Hedda Gabler), she's almost certainly in her late twenties. We're told that she married Torvald eight years ago, and so she must be at least 25, but is unlikely to be over 30: it's important for the play that she's still attractive to Torvald and Rank, and can strike Mrs Linde as a young woman at the peak of her self-confidence and appeal.

It's clear that Nora had a complex relationship with her father. He was evidently a difficult man, who had a reputation for womanising. He was also well off and independent-minded.

Significantly, there is no reference to Nora's mother, and it's likely that she died when Nora was young, perhaps even in childbirth, and that Nora was effectively brought up by her nanny, Anne-Marie. It seems that her father groomed her to act as his attractive consort, almost a child-bride, and this has given her a model for her subsequent behaviour towards her husband. There is no mention of Nora having any brothers or sisters, and Torvald and the children are most probably the complete extent of Nora's surviving family – and so when she leaves, Mrs Linde will be the only person to whom she can turn for help.

Nora's relationship with her husband provides the central dynamic of the play, and it's here that her character is most vividly on display. It's important to take her protestations that she loves Torvald at face value: it was love that made her borrow money from Krogstad, and it's love that makes her want to keep it secret for so long. She's concerned about how Torvald would feel if he discovered that she had saved him and is as worried about losing Torvald as she is about hurting him. Thus it's essential to grasp the extent of Nora's emotional and practical dependence on her husband at the beginning of the play; but also that she understands him better than he does her. Without him she'd have nothing, and the progress of the play is towards an acceptance of that fact and a determination to do without everything that he brings.

Nora uses sexual manipulation as a way of having power over Torvald, but also as a way of pleasing him. But this isn't all one way, and she takes erotic pleasure in it, and in seeing the power that he has over others. She spends much of the play in a state of considerable anxiety, and she often expresses her feelings – and her thoughts – in a kind of febrile agitation (which can be relentless in performance if it's not acted with variation and sophistication). It's important that we should see her childish play as an act (she snaps out of it the moment Torvald leaves the room), but it's rarely perfunctory and should have a real desperation behind it.

Nora takes huge, innocent pleasure in her children, as is evident in the crucial short scene with them in Act One. Although she seems to be a mother who is at ease with her children, she is also trying too hard, racked by deep anxiety about losing them. Her decision to leave Torvald entails losing her children too, and we should recognise that such an act jeopardises any rights she has over them. Nora is no Medea – who kills her children – but she's prepared to sacrifice what she loves for the sake of freedom and truth.

At first glance her attitude towards money is contradictory: she comes into Act One laden with presents and generously tips the porter, bearing out Mrs Linde's memory that she was 'an extravagant little thing at school'. She takes pleasure in money: she's delighted by Torvald's well-paid job and tells Mrs Linde that she daydreams that a 'rich old man [who] was head over heels in love with me' died and left all his money to her in his will. But her attitude comes from familiarity, not ignorance. She's had to learn the hard financial realities, and has proven herself quite capable of paying off her debt to Krogstad out of her housekeeping money, while at the same time maintaining the illusion that she's extravagant. Indeed, her involvement with money plays an essential part in her transformation: 'it was thrilling too, to be sitting there, working, earning money. Almost like a man.'

For much of the play, Nora hides behind a convenient lie – that she's Torvald's 'pretty little thing' – so that she can continue to love him according to his terms. However, the central drama of the play is the transformation in Nora from the child-bride at the beginning into the mature, independent-minded woman of the end. Ibsen himself was quite clear on how he saw her:

> [Nora is] a big, overgrown child, who must go out into the world to discover herself and so may one day be, in due course, fit to raise her children – or maybe not. No one can know. But this much is certain, that with the perspective on marriage that has opened up to her in the course of the night it would be immoral of her to continue living with Helmer: this is impossible for her and this is why she leaves.[19]

Thus the final confrontation with Torvald is the logical conclusion of everything Nora has experienced, however tragic its repercussions might be. She makes her decision more in sorrow than in anger: the woman who leaves at the end is liberated; but she's also all alone in the world.

TORVALD

Torvald Helmer is in the prime of life, perhaps in his mid-thirties although Ibsen doesn't specify his age. Though recently ill, he's now a healthy, confident, successful father of three, married to a beautiful and well-born woman, with a good job, excellent prospects and a comfortable and handsome home.

The most important thing to understand about Torvald is that he's not an immoral man. There isn't the slightest suggestion that he has any of the usual character flaws of the bad husband: alcoholism, violence, abuse or infidelity. He adores his wife and is moved by her presence. A production of the play that presents him as cruel or pathological travesties Ibsen's intentions and unbalances the play. It also makes a nonsense of the real nature of Nora's story.

Torvald is above all utterly conventional and his behaviour is typical of the bourgeois husband of the time. This takes many forms: his presumptions about his own role as the bread-winner and head of the household; his attitudes towards money and debt; his absolute conviction of the rightness of the law at all times;[20] and his patronising attitude to women and what he regards as their world. This shouldn't be satirised in performance: what Ibsen is describing is the 'normal' middle-class *pater familias* of his time. The play demonstrates the limitations of these views, but to pathologise them and make them unique to Torvald defuses its power and meaning.

Ibsen shows that Torvald displays all too real human weaknesses. We gather from Nora that he fell ill because he was working too hard as a lawyer; now we see him taking on the same kind of challenge at the bank, and we cannot be confident that it won't happen again. He treats his wife in very much the same way that he would treat his children: as a silly, sweet thing who shouldn't concern herself with the real matters of the world. The only time she's granted a different role is when he desires her physically, but even then the terms of their erotic relationship revolve around his own pleasure. Torvald looks to Rank as a surrogate father whose friendship and approval is important to him; and he regards Rank's imminent death as a rite of passage that will allow him to be alone with his wife. But above all, Torvald is so wrapped up in himself that he fails to notice what's happening in his own home and is incapable of the kind of profound change – 'the miracle' – that would prevent Nora from walking out on him and their life together.

KROGSTAD

At first glance, Nils Krogstad is little more than a traditional stage villain, the shadowy outsider who threatens the heroine and her happy home, appearing suddenly, frightening children and uttering threats. And indeed, if it's accepted – as it surely should be – that *A Doll's House* isn't entirely free of melodrama, it's at its most evident in Ibsen's presentation of Nora's money-lending blackmailer.

However, we must understand that Krogstad's isolation and bitter sense of injustice make him more than a pantomime villain. Like Shylock in *The Merchant of Venice*, Krogstad has been rejected by the society he wants to join (see, for example, Rank's contemptuous description of him as 'morally sick') and has, in turn, rejected its niceties. Of course the bitter irony – which needs to be made clear in a production – is that the crime that cost him everything is exactly the same as Nora's. Furthermore, Krogstad's under-the-counter money-lending (which has paid for Torvald's health) is nothing more than an unofficial version of Torvald's respected business as a bank manager.

One of the remarkable things about the play is that it shows that Krogstad is capable of redemption – through Mrs Linde's love. Their reconciliation in the first section of Act Three stands in direct counterpoint to Nora and Torvald's separation and demonstrates that Ibsen isn't saying that relationships between men and women are impossible; rather, that the pursuit of individual truth will bring one couple together, even as it drives another apart.

MRS LINDE

Although Kristine Linde's presence gives us the opportunity to hear Nora's backstory, she's much more than simply a 'confidante'.

When we first see Mrs Linde, she's just arrived in town on the steamer (Nora expresses amazement that she's undertaken 'such a long journey, in winter'): she's wearing 'travelling clothes' and exudes a striking independence of mind (Torvald has no hesitation in employing her at the bank). Ibsen deliberately counterpoints her tale of a loveless marriage, selfless devotion and bitter hard work with all the blessings that Nora seems to enjoy: three healthy children, a comfortable home, financial security and Torvald's devotion and love. And, at first, she's condescending to Nora and presumes that she's less experienced in the ways of the world. However, as she discovers more about the nature of Nora's relationship with Torvald, she realises that she's been unfair, while also becoming insistent that Nora should make him face up to the truth.

It's a mistake to see Mrs Linde as a fully formed 'new woman', free of ties and content with a room of her own. She has experienced a great deal of pain and upset. Although she's meant to be the same age as Nora (they were at school together), she walks slowly, saying that she 'finds stairs hard', and knows that her experiences haven't come without a price:

> The worst thing about a situation like mine is that it makes you hard. No one else to work for; always out for yourself; survival, it makes you selfish.

But Ibsen, with his almost Shakespearean sense of paradox and contradiction, shows that it's only love, and love of a fallen man at that, which will give her the reward that she deserves. And it's only through such devotion that her years of struggle can make sense and that she can finally be happy.

RANK

Dr Rank is a deliberately enigmatic figure. Strictly speaking, he belongs to the Scandinavian theatrical tradition of the 'fifth business', the colourful, slightly mysterious, sexually ambivalent stock character who stands aloof from both the main couple and the subplot, but who nevertheless plays a central role in the dramatic action.[21]

Rank has a charm and unconventionality that's attractive to everyone who meets him. At first, it's not explained why such a wealthy and appealing figure should be a rich bachelor who lives by himself. But then it becomes apparent that he's suffering from an unexplained and fatal disease.[22]

Ibsen doesn't specify Rank's age but it's clear that he should be older than Nora and Torvald and may well be in his fifties. He's a close friend of both and visits every day. Torvald finds his approbation and support important in Acts One and Two when, as an experienced man of the world, Rank's sophisticated understanding and confidence rubs off on him. In Act Three, Rank helps him shed some of his inhibitions, secure in the knowledge that any indiscretions will be kept confidential. To Nora, Rank is much more than simply a devoted older man: the two have a flirtatious relationship that only just remains respectable. It's evident, though not fully expressed, that Rank is desperately – almost pathetically – in love with her, not just for her feminine appeal, but also for her energy and independence of mind.

Rank has an intriguing and wry sense of humour and makes light of his imminent death in a way that can be chilling. Joking about next year's fancy dress party he declares that he'll be 'invisible'. When Nora teases him and says that he wants to live, his reply is:

> Most certainly. However dreadful I feel, I want to prolong the agony as long as possible. My patients all feel the same way . . .

Rank knows that his death is imminent, but in his flirtation with Nora, his delight in Torvald's 'dark Havanas' and his playful melancholy, he not only faces up to it with great stoicism, but encourages Torvald to face up to *his* real responsibilities, and, even more importantly, allows Nora to glimpse the possibility of her own renewal.

IVAR, BOB AND EMMY

Nora's 'three beautiful children' have an important role to play, even though we only see them for a brief moment. Although Ibsen has not given their ages, they must be younger than eight, since Nora and Torvald married eight years ago. Nora has done exactly what conventional society expected of her: she's given birth to two sons, Ivar and Bobby; followed by a daughter, Emmy, for contrast.

It's important that a production takes the children seriously, and that the audience is frequently reminded of their existence. The payoff is that at the end of the play, we remember that Nora isn't just leaving her husband, she's abandoning her children, quite possibly for ever. After all, this was a society in which a woman who walks out on her husband without good reason would not be allowed contact with her children.

There are many difficulties associated with working with young children in the theatre, practical as well as artistic, so they are sometimes cut, with only their recorded voices being heard. This is a shame and should be avoided, if possible, though it can be the only practical course of action.

ANNE-MARIE

Anne-Marie was Nora's nanny when she was young, but became much more, almost a surrogate mother. She had to give away her illegitimate child, so that she could take the job: the child's father had left and Anne-Marie was a poor girl 'in trouble'. Since then, she has developed a very close bond with Nora and her children. In leaving her family at the end of the play, Nora is leaving Anne-Marie as much as anyone else. It is a comfort to Nora to know, however, that the children will be well looked after.

HELENE

The part of Helene, the maid, is sometimes amalgamated into that of Anne-Marie. Although this is practical for financial reasons, and gives one actress more to play, Ibsen was clear that he wanted two very different servants – one a youngish maid, and the other an elderly nanny – and there is a real value in making them as distinct as possible. One possibility in English – where dialect says so much – is for Anne-Marie to speak in a peasant, rural accent (which could imply longer service and a different kind of attitude) and for Helene to speak in an urban dialect.

THE PORTER

The Porter works in a department store and carries shopping home for people. He should be pleased by Nora's generous tip: 'keep the change'. This is a tiny part and is sometimes played by a stage manager or an understudy.

Setting

Staging nineteenth-century naturalist drama demands a high level of three-dimensional realism in the location in which the action takes place. Naturalism requires a different approach from the bare stage appropriate for Shakespeare, or the ornamented platform of eighteenth-century drama, let alone the fragmented style advocated by Brecht and adopted by so much contemporary theatre.

Of course, modern designers and directors may want to simplify the setting, to present the poetic essence of the room, or create a more expressionistic setting that interprets the play afresh or releases its subtexts in new or startling ways. A word of warning though: it's difficult for a modern audience to understand the various relationships between the characters in the play without a sense of the world in which they live. In other words, in their search for an original and stylish visualisation of the play, directors and designers need to be careful not to jettison the specific material conditions that create the characters and define what they care about and how they behave.

The action of the three acts of *A Doll's House* is set in one place, the living room of the Helmers' apartment in Christiania. Ibsen's opening stage direction describes in detail what he imagines:

> The decoration is not extravagant, but comfortable and stylish. Back right, door to the hall; back left, door to Helmer's study. Between the doors, a piano. Centre left, a door, and beyond it a window; beside the window a small table, easy chairs and a small sofa. Upstage right, a door, and below it a stove, two easy chairs and a rocking chair. Between the door and the stove, a side-table. Engravings on the walls. A cabinet filled with china and other small objects; a small bookcase with expensively-bound books. Carpet on the floor, fire in the stove.

What's being described is a typical comfortable middle-class home of the time, with all the usual decorations and features. In other words, this is a room that Ibsen's original audiences would have recognised as not unlike their own homes, and in no way special. Furthermore, this is an apartment, not a villa.[23]

When imagining the play on stage it might be a good idea to draw a diagram of this stage direction and get as clear a sense of what Ibsen had in mind as possible. Various things emerge: the door into the hall should be fairly far away from the door to Torvald's study and we need to be able to see the letter box at all times; it's valuable to have a window either to the outside or out in the hallway so that we can get a sense of the time of day; placing the piano against the back wall will help mask the actor at the piano, if the playing has to be mimed; there needs to be a third door, which leads off to the kitchen and the children's area, and it's here that Mrs Linde hides when Krogstad appears. Ibsen has specified two seating areas: the sofa on the one side and the rocking chair and the easy chairs beside the stove. Finally, it's important that we believe that Rank can enter Torvald's study directly from the hall and not have to go through the living room.

In thinking about what a production of the play might look like, it's often useful to find a painter or photographer whose work can give you an appropriate visual language. Ibsen's plays are sometimes interpreted through the filter of Expressionism and Symbolism, and often the paintings of the great Norwegian painter Edvard Munch (1863–1944). Although Munch did know Ibsen (and designed a production of *Ghosts* in 1906), such an approach fails to understand the difference between Ibsen's meticulous naturalism, which frames human beings within the world in which they find themselves, and the internal, expressionist landscapes of Munch's work. More useful, perhaps, is the group of Nordic painters whose work is built on naturalistic observation but allows for deeper meanings to emerge.[24] The domestic paintings of Vilhelm Hammershøi (1864-1916) are particularly useful.[25]

Staging

Ibsen's acute sense of theatrical poetry combined with a practical knowledge of what works in the theatre, means that, when staging his plays, modern actors and directors do well to pay heed to the evidence of his very precise theatrical imagination. His friend Emil Poulson wrote in 1898:

> It is said that he wrote out his plays in his head, down to the minutest detail; only when everything is completely finished is the play written down. Thus he lives with his characters in the most intimate relationship – knows every feature of their faces, every intonation in their voices, virtually every fold in their garments.

Thus it's perhaps useful to see the text more like a film script than a conventional play, in that the spoken words are only part of the overall intention, and sometimes a fairly small part. And like film, meaning is embodied in physical action as much as in the words that are spoken.

STAGE DIRECTIONS

As was common practice at the time, Ibsen's plays were published before they were performed, and he wrote them to be read as well as seen. One of the consequences of this was that he wrote extensive and detailed stage directions, which describe very precisely what he imagined taking place. At first sight these can seem overbearing – too much detail about how a line should be played, where a character should sit and so on – and they're sometimes dismissed as merely the conventions of an outdated theatrical style. Indeed, a production that followed every single stage direction slavishly would almost certainly be a dull one. When reading the play, however, they're very useful in building up a picture of the stage action and shouldn't be ignored.

PACING

The biggest challenge in staging *A Doll's House* is that of pace. The problem is more than simply a question of speed. The difficulty is that Ibsen's dramatic technique relies on the meticulous uncovering of individual characters' backstories, which slowly, and with a crushing sense of inevitability leads step by step to the dramatic crisis. Because Ibsen dispenses with non-naturalistic techniques (above all the soliloquy[26]) it's necessary for this information to be conveyed through lengthy dialogue (for example, Mrs Linde's conversation with Nora in Act One), which often requires stillness and quiet. The best way to prevent this from feeling monotonous is to discover the character's reasons for sharing this information, which will give the actors the necessary drive and imbue the scene with an underlying dramatic tension. Ibsen was acutely aware of the problem and has deliberately built into the play certain 'cliff-hanger' moments when the crucial revelation is interrupted by an unexpected arrival; and he carefully specifies pauses, broken speech and accelerations of pace leading up to dramatic climaxes. Nevertheless, ensuring that *A Doll's House* unfolds at the right pace in the theatre and with appropriate dramatic energy is one of the great challenges facing the director.

PHYSICAL ACTION

It's fundamental to naturalism that the actors should move around the room in a way that's realistic and appropriate. Furthermore, *A Doll's House* often requires a physical stillness, which allows the characters' stories to emerge in the most direct and unostentatious way. The actors shouldn't be asked to demonstrate crude notions about character through their movements and gestures (for example, Krogstad standing tall and proud, Mrs Linde endlessly limping, Nora imitating a doll or a butterfly); a production should trust the dramatic power of what's said and done to carry the evening. Nevertheless, it's a mistake to imagine that the play should just become 'talking heads'; Ibsen has deliberately included a number of highly sophisticated theatrical moments, which embody the meaning of the play in the most vivid way imaginable. These are highlighted as they occur in *The Action* (see page 28).

A NOTE ON THE TARANTELLA

At the climax of Act Two, Nora dances a tarantella, a traditional Italian peasant dance for women to cure them of the bite of the tarantula (which would, according to legend, otherwise turn them into a werewolf). It was also derived from the movements of a woman trying to cure herself of feelings of depression and frustration at her subordinate position in life. The Neapolitan tarantella has a particularly wild and whirling movement and is often portrayed being danced beneath the smoking Vesuvius. As such it expresses the peculiarly Neapolitan juxtaposition of catastrophe with pleasure and embodies Nora's unfulfilled, and dangerous, yearning for freedom. It's very likely that Ibsen would have seen Italians dancing the tarantella in Amalfi, where he wrote *A Doll's House*.

The tarantella has a rapid 6/8 metre, with an ever-increasing tempo, and this escalation of physical and psychological energy produces an eventual release – not unlike orgasm – that clears the dancer of the actual or metaphorical poison that's burning in her blood. Thus Ibsen's choice of the tarantella is particular, and on stage it's a perfect image of Nora's soul struggling to be free.

Lighting

The naturalist movement in art – inspired by Dutch domestic painting as well as the Impressionists – was fascinated by the play of light on everyday objects. The coming of naturalistic drama coincided with the invention of electric lighting in the 1880s, which, though crude by modern standards, transformed what was possible in the theatre.

The naturalists maintained that physical and material conditions – weather, hours of daylight, cold, heat and so on – are all instrumental in the forging of character, and Ibsen's first naturalist masterpiece is no exception. A Doll's House *is set in the depths of the Norwegian winter and climate is fundamental to the play's atmosphere and meaning. Everybody involved in a production of the play should bear in mind certain realities: Christiania, where the play is set, is very far north (further north than anywhere in Britain) and the average midwinter temperature is -6°C with a high probability of snow. Hours of daylight are very limited: the sun rises at ten in the morning and sets at about three in the afternoon. These physical conditions have a profound effect on behaviour, and it's impossible to understand the action of the play without an awareness of them.*

In the modern theatre the lighting can be very precise and evocative of a specific quality; the play benefits enormously from the careful attention of a skilful and imaginative lighting designer.

The play takes place over three consecutive days, at three different times of day.

ACT ONE

It is late morning on Christmas Eve. The light we see through the front door, and shining through the windows in the apartment, is brilliantly white – cold and fresh. This is emphasised by being reflected off the snow. Mrs Linde, just off the steamer from the North, provides a bracing breath of fresh air – and a sharp dose of cold reality.

ACT TWO

Act Two takes place in the afternoon of Christmas Day. It opens with daylight coming in through the windows but fading rapidly. The maid brings in lamps just at the moment that Nora's flirtation with Dr Rank is in danger of going too far, and their arrival casts light on their illicit relationship. The atmosphere that has been building up through the act becomes increasingly oppressive and claustrophobic, leading to the climax: the rehearsal of the tarantella.

ACT THREE

The last act takes place in the middle of the night on Boxing Day. The stove is blazing hot; Torvald and Rank have been warmed by champagne, as has Nora by dancing the tarantella. The heat inside the flat deliberately contrasts with the cold night outside: a world of empty streets, falling snow and freezing black water, in which Nora imagines drowning herself. When she finally leaves, we should be able to imagine her walking beneath a bright full moon and a brilliant canopy of stars: cold, sharp and free.

Costumes

Costume details express the material and social position of the characters in a way that is both meaningful and poetic. They can also express a great deal about a character's taste, sense of style and self-image.

A Doll's House *is nearly always produced in 'period costume', namely those worn in late nineteenth-century Christiania.[27] They should convey all the sobriety and respectability of the Scandinavian middle class of the time.*

It's important to remember that the play takes place in deep winter and that all the characters should wear hats, coats and gloves whenever they venture outdoors or come into the apartment from outside.

NORA

The actress playing Nora should have at least three different costumes.

In Acts One and Two, she should wear the smart day clothes of a highly respectable, middle-class wife. These could be fresh in tone and distinguish her from the much drabber clothes that everyone else wears. She deliberately dresses prettily and fairly expensively, and her clothes should show her good figure to its best advantage. It's possible that she wears a more festive dress on Christmas Day.

For the fancy dress party in Act Three, Nora wears a Neapolitan fishing girl's costume: this should be garish, almost pornographic, like something from an entirely different world. Its bright colours and revealing cut would be distinctly out of place in nineteenth-century Norway and they represent the low point of Nora's humiliation. This is, of course, the same garment that we see Mrs Linde repairing in Act Two.

Finally, at the end of Act Three, Nora changes her clothes once again, into the sober practical outfit of the independent woman, and her psychological metamorphosis should be reflected in this final physical transformation.

TORVALD

Torvald's costume in Acts One and Two should indicate his new position in society. His clothes should be carefully looked after at all times: his frock coat black, his shirt starched, and he should have the studs, cufflinks and fob watch of the successful bourgeois.

In Act Three, Torvald wears white tie and tails, and a large, swirling, black cloak, which Nora wraps around her when she contemplates suicide. It's possible that he even wears a mask, and for a moment looks like a figure from the Neapolitan Carnival when he first appears in the Act.

THE CHILDREN

The three children should be well turned out, as befits the children of a Bank Manager. The oldest son, Ivar, might be dressed in a child's naval uniform. The sight of the three together should exert a conventional charm and appeal.

MRS LINDE

Ibsen writes that when Mrs Linde first arrives she's wearing 'travelling clothes'. Her costume should tell the story of her recent arrival in town – possibly mud-spattered, or wet from brushing against snow – as well as being suggestive of an independent-minded, self-sufficient woman (such as a bank clerk or a secretary). Although born to the same class as Nora, her clothes should suggest hard work and poverty. Furthermore, she's a widow and should probably wear black. There should be a striking contrast between her modest and practical clothes and Nora's feminine and expensive outfit.

KROGSTAD

Krogstad's clothes should be simple: probably a black suit, white shirt, and black tie. His costume should show his poverty, but should also reflect his desire to be respectable and accepted. It would be a mistake to dress Krogstad in clothes that make him look particularly sinister: down-at-heel ordinariness is the key.

RANK

Dr Rank's clothes should give a clear sense of his bachelor wealth and his professional status as a doctor; it's also worth considering whether they could convey something of his colourful eccentricity (such as a flamboyant waistcoat in Act Three). Otherwise his clothes should be predominantly black and white, with gold and silver reserved for his cufflinks, a fob watch, a ring and so on.

HELENE AND ANNE-MARIE

Helene should wear a middle-class maid's uniform. Anne-Marie's clothes are more personal, and less formal, and can reflect her age and closeness to the family.

Props and Furniture

Ibsen is very particular about the props and furniture that are required. All these objects need to carry the details of nineteenth-century Scandinavian interiors, but they should also be designed in such a way that they convey essential dramatic meaning.

MACAROONS

At the beginning of Act One, Nora carries a little bag of macaroons – small and very sweet almond biscuits – and eats two of them. These reflect Nora's playful, happy-go-lucky mood, and deliberately suggest to Torvald and the audience her childish, extravagant taste.

CHRISTMAS PRESENTS

At the beginning of Act One, Nora has bought Christmas presents for her family and Ibsen specifies what these should be: 'A new outfit for Ivar, and a little sword. A horse and a trumpet for Bob. A doll and a doll's bed for Emmy . . . Dress-lengths and hankies for the maids.' These haven't come from the most expensive shops, but from careful bargain hunting ('Nothing expensive: they'll soon be broken anyway'). They're individually wrapped, but not in Christmas paper: the shop-keeper would wrap each item, probably in brown paper and string, when they were bought.

CHRISTMAS TREE

When the Christmas tree first appears in Act One it should look freshly cut down and 'untrimmed'. It was regarded as unlucky to put a tree up before Christmas Eve, and once decorated, with real candles and little presents wrapped in golden paper, it was taken down at the end of Christmas Day.[28] The tree itself shouldn't be very tall – after all Helene is meant to bring it on by herself and put it in the middle of the room[29] – but it's important to remember that the Norwegians are very particular about Christmas trees and treat their symbolism with respect. In Act Two the tree is shorn of its decorations with the candles all burnt down and is left in the corner of the room. By Act Three it has disappeared.

TAMBOURINE

Nora strikes a tambourine to accompany herself in the rehearsal for the tarantella in Act Two. This should be Italian in design, and have a visual connection with her fishing-girl costume. In Southern Italy, there is a variation on the tambourine known as the 'Tamburella' (slightly bigger and more Roman in feel), and it's possible that Nora should use one of these. She should probably bring it with her on stage into Act Three, to help us visualise what has taken place upstairs at the fancy dress party.

LETTERS AND DOCUMENTS

It's important that the various letters and documents – above all, Krogstad's letters to Torvald and the original contract between Krogstad and Nora – should be carefully designed and credible: this was a world before telephones and computers, and the written word was legally binding. When Torvald returns from the bank at the end of Act One he should carry a portfolio containing the proposed staffing review at the bank. Again, this should be an object of considerable bureaucratic importance.

LETTER BOX

Ibsen specifies that the front door to the Helmers' apartment should have a letter box with a lockable cage on the inside, which can only be opened by Torvald, who holds the key. This shouldn't be seen as evidence of any control mania on Torvald's behalf; it would have been entirely normal in a middle-class apartment. It's very important that the audience should be able to see at all times what is – and is not – in the letter box.

VISITING CARDS

In late nineteenth-century Europe, gentlemen – and some ladies too – would carry personalised visiting cards (not unlike modern business cards), which they would give to servants to announce their visit, and leave behind if the person they had visited was not there. The fact that the name of the visitor does not need to be said is used by Ibsen to great dramatic effect, especially in Act Two when Krogstad gives his visiting card to the maid to give to Nora, who is ensconced with Rank; Nora tells Rank that it's the dressmaker, but we – and Rank – can guess from her reaction that it's someone more important. In Act Three, Rank deposits two visiting cards – one for Nora and one for Helmer – marked with a black cross: an elegant way of announcing his own intention to stay in his apartment for the last days before his death.

THE STOVE

In Scandinavian countries with their bitterly cold winters, before the invention of oil-fired and electric central heating, large wood-burning stoves (not used for cooking) were a vital piece of domestic equipment. The floor to ceiling stove in *A Doll's House* is the only source of warmth in the living room, and the obvious focal point for intimate conversations. It also has a symbolic role in the play: it's the eternal flame of the Vestal virgin (Nora herself), and the instrument of purgative destruction (Torvald burns Krogstad's letters and contracts in the stove).[30]

THE ROCKING CHAIR

The rocking chair by the stove with its easy, relaxing movement is an ideal place for a kind of isolated, ruminative exploration of the past, and it's used as such on several occasions. While it might have a small cushion on its seat, this should be a simple item and not especially comfortable. There should also be a simple wooden chair, or perhaps a stool, beside the rocking chair, so that conversations can take place at the stove.

THE SOFA

This provides an ideal location for the more intimate and dramatic conversations. It's possible that it is the most elegant object in the room. It shouldn't be too big, so that when two people sit on it – for example, Rank and Nora – they're necessarily in some proximity with each other. By modern standards, it'll be a fairly uncomfortable, upright affair.

A TABLE AND TWO CHAIRS

In Act Three, Ibsen specifies that a table and two chairs should be brought into the room. Although it's unclear as to why – perhaps Torvald and Nora have used them for an early dinner before the fancy dress party – they provide a superb focus for both Mrs Linde and Krogstad's reconciliation and Torvald and Nora's final confrontation.

WEDDING RINGS

As Nora places her wedding ring on the table that stands between her and her husband, and asks for his ring to be given back to her, we see that their marriage is definitely over. The golden ring should glow against the dark wood of the table. The image will be that much more clearer and more potent if the table has nothing else on it.

Sound and Music

In the naturalist theatre, sound carries as much information as material objects. A Doll's House was written before the invention of recorded sound, so the effects that are required are easily achievable, but need to be carefully considered.

The play has very little need of music – except for the tarantella – and it's preferable that this should be the only music used (which will give it greater impact). The use of loud music between the acts can make the nuances and delicacy of the dialogue feel pale and insubstantial by contrast.

FRONT DOORBELL

Ibsen asks for the doorbell to be heard on two or three occasions. Although in the last act this produces an enormously dramatic effect, the bell itself should be perfectly ordinary, indicating an entirely predictable, well-regulated household.

PIANO MUSIC FOR THE TARANTELLA

For an idea of what the music for the tarantella sounds like, readers can visit the following websites:

http://www.dieli.net/SicilyPage/Folksongs/folkmusic.html
http://www.sicilianculture.com/folklore/tarantella.htm

THE PARTY UPSTAIRS

While Krogstad and Mrs Linde are talking to each other at the beginning of Act Three we should hear the noise of the party in the apartment upstairs. We should also hear muffled laughter, voices, people walking around, and perhaps some dancing. There could be some music playing – probably a piano – building up to the tune for the tarantella, the same music that Rank played at the end of Act Two. This would give the atmosphere of an enjoyable, light-hearted but over-heated party. The sound should both echo the turmoil in Nora's heart and contrast with the sober and life-changing mood of Krogstad and Mrs Linde's reconciliation.

FRONT DOOR AND THE HALL

It's worthwhile thinking about the noises that can be heard from the hallway between the front door of the apartment and the door into the living room. It's obviously vital that when we hear the sound of Nora slamming the door behind her for the last time, we understand what is happening.

The final sound of the play ('A door slams, off') is one of the most famous in theatre history (along with the mysterious effect required in Act Two of Chekhov's *The Cherry Orchard*[31]). There should be two distinct noises: first, the front door of the apartment shutting, and then the door to the apartment block – presumably one floor beneath – slamming shut. This marks the climax of Ibsen's great drama of transformation and liberation, which not only ushered in a new kind of theatre, but, many say, helped to shape the modern world.

Endnotes

1　One of the peculiar pleasures – and challenges – of approaching *A Doll's House* today is realising just how big an impact the play has already made on the audience coming to see it – even if some of them have never seen it, or even heard of it, before.

2　Letter to Lucie Wolf from Ibsen 25 May 1883. Quoted in James McFarlane (ed.), *Henrik Ibsen. A Critical Anthology* (Harmondsworth: Penguin, 1970).

3　The key figures in the evolution of the naturalist novel are Émile Zola, Gustave Flaubert, Honoré de Balzac, Leo Tolstoy, Ivan Turgenev, Fyodor Dostoevsky, Charles Dickens and George Eliot. The most important naturalist painter was Gustave Courbet, but naturalism had a huge impact on the Impressionists: Camille Pissarro, Edgar Degas, Claude Monet, Pierre Renoir and Paul Cézanne.

4　Ibsen's association is one of the selling points of what is now a luxury seaside hotel.

5　Kate Millett, *Sexual Politics* (New York: Doubleday, 1970).

6　Joan Templeton, *Ibsen's Women* (Cambridge: Cambridge University Press, 1997).

7　This kind of campaigning, issue-based drama is more characteristic of three of Ibsen's British admirers, George Bernard Shaw, John Galsworthy and Harley Granville-Barker, whose plays constantly tussle with broad social issues – unemployment, prostitution, social justice, education, and so on – often to remarkable effect.

8　James McFarlane (ed.), *Henrik Ibsen. A Critical Anthology* (Harmondsworth: Penguin, 1970).

9　Many of Shakespeare's plays do the same thing: in *King Lear* one old man (Lear) goes mad because of the ingratitude and cruelty of his daughters; the other (Gloucester) loses his eyes and gains new sight because of his sons. It is the combination of the two stories that gives the play its depth and reality.

10　In 1880 the population of what is now Norway was less than two million and the population of Christiania was less than 40,000, the size of a small seaside town in modern Britain.

11 Between 1825 and 1925, 800,000 Norwegians emigrated to the United States. The subject of immigration is explored in Ibsen's *Pillars of the Community*.

12 The original Norwegian title literally means 'a doll's home', and some argue that the standard English translation fails to reflect the sense of a home being lived in by a doll: the English suggests a house for several dolls, and the distinction between the plural (dolls') and the singular (doll's) is not heard. Having said that, it is difficult to work out a better title: possibly *The Doll's Home*. Obviously, this is a decision to be made by the individual translator.

13 See for example Ingmar Bergman's remarkable TV series *Scenes from a Marriage* (1973), which is quite explicitly influenced by *A Doll's House*.

14 There is potential for confusion here. Torvald is still a lawyer – a barrister, indeed – although, as a bank manager, he is no longer practising law. This overlapping of the professions would have been much more common then.

15 Which is where Ibsen wrote much of *A Doll's House*.

16 This is sometimes translated as 'decorated': Ibsen's intention, it seems, is both 'trimmed' (i.e. cut into shape) *and* 'decorated'.

17 From *Notes for a Tragedy for Today* (1880), quoted in James McFarlane (ed.), *Henrik Ibsen. A Critical Anthology* (Harmondsworth: Penguin, 1970).

18 Sigmund Freud was fascinated with the notion of 'female hysteria' and wrote several case studies – most famously *Dora* – which investigated the condition. The same idea appears in *King Lear*.

19 Letter from Ibsen to Erik af Adholm in Robert Ferguson, *Henrik Ibsen: A New Biography* (London: Richard Cohen Books, 1996).

20 As a qualified lawyer, Torvald is particularly concerned about any association with petty criminality.

21 Ibsen used this convention extensively. See, for example, Judge Brack in *Hedda Gabler*, Jakob Engstrand in *Ghosts*, Brendel in *Rosmersholm*, The Rat Wife in *Little Eyolf* and so on.

22 This is probably inherited syphilis, as suggested by Nora in Act Two: 'He's seriously ill. Lesions in the spine. Poor man. His father was horrible. Woman after woman. That's why the son. . . tainted blood.' Osvald in Ibsen's next play, *Ghosts*, is suffering from the same disease. Both plays are

concerned with the notion of the sins of the father being
visited on the child.

23 Compare this with *Hedda Gabler*, which takes place in a
villa; in other words, a much more expensive place to live.

24 See for example: *Northern Light: Nordic Art at the Turn of
the Century* by Kirk Varnedoe.

25 I should acknowledge, of course, that Hammershøi is a year
younger than Munch and equally anachronistic. However,
his paintings of women sitting alone, often with their backs
to the viewer, in simple, airy rooms, provided the set
designer Bunny Christie and me with what seemed a
perfect visual corollary for our production of *A Doll's House*.

26 There are moments in *A Doll's House* when Nora is left
alone on stage, and she even sometimes says a word or two,
but these are written to be staged as naturalistic action:
people in moments of stress do occasionally talk to
themselves, and there should be no evident awareness of
the audience.

27 Of course, it's legitimate to stage the play in modern
costumes, but it would be important to resolve the contradiction between the modern setting and the specifically
late nineteenth century issues that the play raises.

28 For an image of a nineteenth-century Scandinavian
Christmas, see Ingmar Bergman's great film *Fanny and
Alexander* (1982).

29 In my production, the very short tree was taller than the
even shorter elderly actress (Ina McCarthy, now sadly dead)
who played the maid; we all laughed when in the technical
rehearsal she came on carrying the tree – it looked like a
very small Birnam Wood advancing on Dunsinane in Act
Five of *Macbeth*.

30 The stove is also the means of destruction in Ibsen's other
work: Hedda destroys Løvborg's manuscript in the stove in
Hedda Gabler.

31 'They all remain seated, deep in thought. The only sound
is that of old Firs, muttering as usual. Suddenly a far-off
noise is heard, as if in the heavens – like the sound of a
breaking string, dying away, sadly.' *The Cherry Orchard*,
Drama Classics edition, Nick Hern Books, 2000, page 46.